Historical Criticism of the Bible

Historical Criticism of the Bible

Methodology or Ideology?

Eta Linnemann

Translated from the German edition,

Wissenschaft oder Meinung? Anfragen und Alternativen

by Robert W. Yarbrough

BAKER BOOK HOUSE
Grand Rapids, Michigan 49516

ISBN: 0-8010-5662-4

Fifth printing, January 1995

Printed in the United States of America

Library of Congress Cataloging-in-Publication Data
Linnemann, Eta.
  [Wissenschaft oder Meinung? English]
  Historical criticism of the Bible: methodology or ideology?/Eta
Linnemann; translated from the German edition by Robert W. Yarbrough.
      p.   cm.
  Translation of: Wissenschaft oder Meinung?
  ISBN 0-8010-5662-4
  1. Bible—Evidences, authority, etc. 2. Apologetics—20th century. 3.
Bible—Hermeneutics. 4. Evangelicalism—Doctrines. 5. Word of God (Theology)
6. Linnemann, Eta. I. Title.
  BT1102.L4913   1990
  220.6'01—dc20
                                                        90-34958
                                                             CIP
Originally published in German under the title Wissenschaft oder Meinung?
Anfragen und Alternativen by Hänssler-Verlag (Friedrich Hänssler KG, Bis-
marckstr. 4, D-7303 Neuhausen, West Germany, 1986). All rights reserved.

    Footnotes in brackets ([ ]) indicate material that has been added for clarifi-
cation by the translator.

Contents

Translator's Introduction

This book presents the reader with a challenge—and a treat. When in November 1988 I presented a paper on Eta Linnemann at a professional meeting, discussing her contribution to New Testament studies and her current views as expressed in this book, four publishers expressed interest in it. This is an indication, I think, of the high level of appeal and relevance of Dr. Linnemann's study.

For one thing, there is a fascinating personal dimension which gives the book depth and poignancy. Linnemann lodges a strong protest against the tendencies and methods of a discipline which she knows from the inside out. She is not taking potshots from afar; she was a diligent and receptive student of some of this century's truly seminal thinkers in German New Testament scholarship: Bultmann, Fuchs, Gogarten, and Ebeling. Later, inducted into the world's most prestigious professional society for New Testament research, she was the peer of many others of like stature.

What would possess someone to renounce such achievement? Why would someone literally throw in the trash all of the books and articles she had toiled to see published? Why would anyone give up a position in the West German university system to serve, eventually, as a missionary teacher in Indonesia? This book furnishes at least the broad outlines of the answers to these and other intriguing questions.

But Linnemann's presentation is gripping from more than the human interest angle. Her personal story is ultimately but the vehicle for substantial ruminations on the history, methods, and results of what she calls, with considerable justification, *historical-critical theology*. Here, perhaps, lies the main significance of Linnemann's reflections.

It is here also that one encounters the book's challenge, a challenge that extends to several levels. On the first level the non-German reader will find certain sections dealing with a situation that probably seems foreign. This will be especially true for chapter 4 and the two excurses following. Here Linnemann wrestles with the need for, the possibility of, and basic steps toward the formation of university-level Christian colleges in West Germany.

It is not that there are no Bible colleges whatsoever in German-speaking Western Europe; one can find these in such West German or Swiss locations as Adelshofen, Beatenberg, Brake, Seeheim, Wiedenest, Wölmersen, and Wuppertal, to name only a few. It is rather that these Bible colleges do not offer training at as high an academic level as the theological education offered in the theology faculties of the state universities. Nor are these Bible institutes accorded the same official recognition as that enjoyed by the state schools. What American readers take for granted—the existence of dozens of accredited Christian liberal arts colleges and even some universities that are at least nominally Christian—is nonexistent in the country most familiar to Linnemann, West Germany. Linnemann, and many along with her, feel that the monopoly of the state universities over the training of Germany's pastors, religion teachers, theologians, and biblical scholars has had negative, even disastrous, effects in the last two hundred years.

Yet, while the situation that exercises Linnemann may at first sound strange to many readers, her comments are by no means irrelevant in America where fully accredited Christian colleges are a fact of life. The questions she entertains—what is truly Christian higher education, and how can Christians go about pursuing it more effectively and more biblically in a world dominated by fundamentally atheistic academic institutions?—are often asked at American Christian colleges which are not too reactionary to be concerned with assimilating contemporary learning or too complacently sophisticated to realize how much their worldview concedes to an anti-Christian *Zeitgeist*.

On a second level some will find the book challenging because they are familiar with the history of ideas Linnemann critiques. Especially in chapter 1, and at other points as well, one encounters a wide range of thinkers, perhaps a wider sampling than might be expected in a book penned by someone trained primarily in New Testament criticism. Some might see this as a weakness, asking why Linnemann does not confine herself to the discipline in which she has undoubted expertise. The nature of her reflections and proposals, however, requires that she lift her gaze, and that of her readers, beyond the narrow confines of a particular academic discipline. Linnemann's discussion is wide-ranging to encompass her concerns and what we might call her burden. Those who question the relevance of, say, Goethe to modern hermeneutics (see chapter 1) might consult Jaroslav Pelikan, who sees in Goethe's *Faust* "the classic dramatization both of the positive and of the negative relations between 'Christian doctrine and modern culture.'"[1] If Linnemann has erred in attempting an analysis of the relation between scientific method and biblical interpretation within the context of the history of ideas, she is in good company.

On a third level what we have called Linnemann's burden will present a challenge, if not a stone of stumbling, to some. Quite deliberately Linnemann is *not* writing a formal academic treatise as such,[2] but rather a *Bußruf*—a call to repentance. This might disappoint those wishing for more expositional subtlety, fuller academic content, and a milder tone. Such readers should look forward to Linnemann's next book. It might annoy others who do not like the sound of preaching, especially when it seems to be directed their way and accompanied by the sheer volume of Scripture which Linnemann cites.

It is not the purpose here to seek to justify the manner of address Linnemann has chosen, but it might be well to keep a couple of considerations in view, lest impatience with form prevent sober contemplation of content:

First, it should be remembered that the occasionally zealous tone is perfectly understandable, given the monstrous nature and scope of the deception against which Linnemann sees herself working. Even if the times are only half as perilous as Linnemann thinks, she would have been negligent to mince words or confine herself to a more soothing tone. Other writers in the history of Christian thought have likewise found that drastic error calls for forceful address.

Second, one should bear in mind the circumstances of Linnemann's conversion and preceding years of what she now sees as false teaching (see her Introduction). No doubt it was

1. Jaroslav Pelikan, *The Christian Tradition*, Vol. 5: *Christian Doctrine and Modern Culture (since 1700)* (Chicago/London: University of Chicago Press, 1989), 1.

2. She is engaged in writing an academically oriented work which will cover some of the same ground, but in a more in-depth fashion and from a different perspective, than this popularly written one.

with verve and conviction that she urged students in bygone days that the Bible contains many errors, that miracles are not and never were possible, and that only critical "scientific" methodology is capable of rendering a responsible verdict on the meaning of a biblical text. It would be unrealistic for readers to expect Linnemann to exhibit less *élan* in promulgating truth than she once showed in spreading error; it would be hypocritical of her to do so.

Third, it is at least possible that Linnemann correctly asserts that the current malaise in Western theology—which may not be totally unrelated to pressing dilemmas in Western society at large—calls for repentance, not simply further research, dialogue, or critical reflection. In calling for repentance, it is worth noting that she is only preaching what she has personally practiced. If Linnemann has gone astray in singling out repentance (and a committed posture toward God's written Word and Messiah) as integral to recovering spiritual and moral direction in a deeply troubled world, she once more has plenty of prophetic company in the history of Judeo-Christian proclamation.

Fourth, readers who find the use of scripture overdone at points can congratulate themselves that they know the Bible so well that citations are redundant. One more reading of familiar texts will do no harm, and may yield new treasures in the novel settings in which Linnemann applies them. If there ever was a time when the American public knew the Bible intimately, that time is now over. For many readers the texts Linnemann cites will be unfamiliar. This is certainly true for the European audience Linnemann had in mind when she first wrote.

These are some factors, then, which are worth noting in coming to grips with the tone of Linnemann's work. Even if someone may take exception here and there, such considerations may assist in making a constructive assessment of the arguments marshaled.

A fourth level of challenge may be Linnemann's generally black depiction of the current state of biblical scholarship, and the drastic prescription she proposes for change. Is she not overstating her case?

It is important to bear in mind that her primary frame of reference is West Germany and the university system there. Those familiar with that context and its counterpart in North America can vouch for the veracity of her general thesis that theological and biblical research is indeed most often pursued under atheistic auspices. That is, it is not the true and living God, and his revealed Word, the Bible, that are the focal point of theological reflection. In the modern world, as Linnemann rightly notes, God is unknowable, and revelation in its traditional definition is no longer acceptable or valid. The focus of theology is instead human experience as defined by the theories of modern social science, philosophy, historiography, and other "scientific" disciplines. "God," as understood in historic orthodox Christian thought, is systematically ruled out of consideration and is replaced by human self-awareness and purely immanent forces; as the historical theology textbooks put it, anthropology replaces theology.

Given this milieu, which Linnemann knows intimately because of her own past commitment to it, she understandably tends to state her case in black-white terms. While some remarks may be somewhat more applicable to the European scene, it should be noted that outside of the relatively small world of evangelical scholarship in North America the same academic rules apply. Much, indeed most, theological and biblical research proceeds under assumptions that are not amenable to historic orthodox Christian understanding of God, man, and their relationship as described in the Bible.

Therefore, Linnemann's somewhat grim assessment of the present situation and her radical prescription for change may be utterly relevant to the North American scene. Much of what she says does indeed apply to nonevangelical scholarship and institutions—which train a very large portion of North America's pastors and theological educators. And it also has direct relevance for the evangelical community in at least two ways.

First, evangelical scholarship is undoubtedly influenced by the atheistic academic world that Linnemann describes. It is often assumed that the effect of this is benign; as long as evangelicals maintain pious hearts and upright lives, what goes into their heads, or what they propound as critical theory, is of secondary importance. But this is surely a shortsighted view of things: Atheistic scholarship's effects are in fact not always benign, as one can readily observe from the doctrinal and moral confusion today rampant in churches whose leaders and members have for decades been indoctrinated by this scholarship.

Liberals themselves are expressing disenchantment today with the God they have long preached, and some are calling for a return to a "biblically informed vision" of God, church, and world.[3]

Second, evangelicals can ill afford to be complacent about where their own scholarship, influenced as it is by the larger academic world, is taking them. There has been no shortage of voices in recent years—one thinks of such varied spokesmen as the late Francis Schaeffer, Carl F. H. Henry, and James D. Hunter[4]—who express the conviction that evangelicalism is, so to speak, living on borrowed time and drifting in an unhealthy direction.[5] Christian higher education plays a strategic role here, for good or for ill. Moreover, it has been plausibly alleged that even evangelical theological education is, if not in crisis, then not far from it.[6] At the more popular level few evangelical leaders would be so bold as to assert that the present moral state of theologically conservative churches and their leadership is beyond reproof. In such a situation Linnemann's diagnosis and prescription have preemptive value, calling evangelicals to consider their ways before current maladies escalate to fatal proportions—assuming, of course, that it is not already too late.

Critical reviewers and readers at large are likely to find much in what follows that is disturbing, and some with which they will take absolute exception. But they are sure to encounter much, too, that is absolutely true, much that will stimulate profitable reflection in the lives of students, teachers, church leaders, and seekers after truth in general.

My thanks to Allan Fisher, Linda Triemstra, and Paul Ingram

3. William McKinney, "From the Center to the Margin," *Books & Religion* 16:1 (1989), 3. For a liberal call for renewed attention to the Bible in theological education see, for example, W. Brueggemann, "The Case for an Alternative Reading," *Theological Education* 23 (1987): 89–107. Criticizing liberalism's (but also evangelicalism's) unreal God from within the liberal community is Joanne Swenson, "Treating God as Real," *Theology Today* (October 1988): 446–50.

4. Francis Schaeffer, *The Great Evangelical Disaster* (Westchester, Ill.: Crossway, 1984); Carl F. H. Henry, *Twilight of a Great Civilization* (Westchester Ill.: Crossway, 1988); James D. Hunter, *Evangelicalism: The Coming Generation* (Chicago: University of Chicago Press, 1987).

5. As a sociologist Hunter does not call evangelicalism's apparent future face "unhealthy," but he does think he can document a liberal drift.

6. Scott J. Hafemann, "Seminary, Subjectivity, and the Centrality of Scripture," *Journal of the Evangelical Theological Society* 31 (1988): 129–43.

of Baker Book House for their interest and editorial support, and to Dr. Linnemann for her diligence, thoroughness, and graciousness in overseeing this translation. Remaining ambiguities and infelicities of expression should be charged to the account of the translator and not the author.

Robert W. Yarbrough
Wheaton College
Wheaton, Illinois
July 5, 1989

Preface

I was not alone in writing this book; many loyal friends worked alongside me through their prayers. Most of all I wish to mention my church in Leer, West Germany, especially Brother Hans-Peter Grabe, who serves as leader of the congregation. Not only did he labor as an intercessor before the Lord; through his repeated encouragements he contributed to the book's inception. Thanks are due likewise to my colleagues in the mission agency *Christus für Dich* ("Christ for You") and to my sister in the Lord Gertrud Scholz, who both prayed for the book and rendered valuable assistance in proofreading.

In addition, I should like to mention my church in Odenwald, West Germany, with its leader, Erling Eichholz, and the prayer circle headed up by Sister Elisabeth Hettinger. Thanks are due also to my sisters in the Lord Lilot Schöller and Ruth Parasie and my brothers Gerhard Ullrichs and Martin Schwarz.

My thanks to all of these, as well as to the prayer team at Hänssler-Verlag and to all those not mentioned here by name. I am grateful to Friedrich Hänssler for his willingness to accept the book for publication.

I would also like to thank Dr. R. Yarbrough, who has done a fine job of translating, and Baker Book House, who have been willing to make the book available for English-speaking readers.

Dr. Eta Linnemann
Batu, Indonesia
June 1, 1989

Author's Introduction

"Why do you say 'No!' to historical-critical theology?" I have been confronted with this question, and I wish to state at the outset: My "No!" to historical-critical theology stems from my "Yes!" to my wonderful Lord and Savior Jesus Christ and to the glorious redemption he accomplished for me on Golgotha.

As a student of Rudolf Bultmann and Ernst Fuchs, as well as Friedrich Gogarten and Gerhard Ebeling, I had the best professors which historical-critical theology could offer to me. And I did not do too badly in other respects, either. My first book turned out to be a best-seller. I became professor of theology and religious education at Braunschweig Technical University, West Germany. Upon completing the rigorous requirements for a university lectureship,[1] I was awarded the title of honorary professor of New Testament in the theology faculty of Philipps University, Marburg, West Germany. I was inducted into the Society for New Testament Studies. I had the satisfaction of an increasing degree of recognition from my colleagues.

Intellectually comfortable with historical-critical theology, I was deeply convinced that I was rendering a service to God with my theological work and contributing to the proclamation of the gospel. Then, however, on the basis of various observations, discoveries, and a resulting self-awareness, I was forced to concede two things I did not wish: (1) no "truth" could emerge from this "scientific work on the biblical text," and (2) such labor does not serve the proclamation of the gospel. At the time this was just a practical realization emerging from experiences which I could no longer deny. Since then, God through his grace and Word has given me insight into the theoretical dimensions of this theology. Instead of being based on God's Word, it had its foun-

---

1. [Linnemann refers to her *Habilitationschrift*, a scholarly writing which in the USA would amount to something very much like a second doctoral dissertation. It qualifies one to lecture in the German university.]

dations in philosophies which made bold to define truth so that God's Word was excluded as the source of truth. These philosophies simply presupposed that man could have no valid knowledge of the God of the Bible, the Creator of heaven and earth, the Father of our Savior and Lord Jesus Christ.

Today I realize that historical-critical theology's monopolistic character and world-wide influence is a sign of God's judgment (Rom. 1:18–32). God predicted this in his Word: "For the time will come when men will not put up with sound doctrine. Instead, to suit their own desires, they will gather around them a great number of teachers to say what their itching ears want to hear" (2 Tim. 4:3). He also promised to send "a powerful delusion so that they will believe the lie" (2 Thess. 2:11). *God is not dead, nor has he resigned. He reigns, and he is already executing judgment on those who declare him dead or assert that he is a false god who does nothing, either good or evil.*

Today I know that I owe those initial insights to the beginning effects of God's grace. At first, however, what I realized led me into profound disillusionment. I reacted by drifting toward addictions which might dull my misery. I became enslaved to watching television and fell into an increasing state of alcohol dependence. My bitter personal experience finally convinced me of the truth of the Bible's assertion: "Whoever finds his life will lose it" (Matt. 10:39). At that point God led me to vibrant Christians who knew Jesus personally as their Lord and Savior. I heard their testimonies as they reported what God had done in their lives. Finally God himself spoke to my heart by means of a Christian brother's words. By God's grace and love I entrusted my life to Jesus.

He immediately took my life into his saving grasp and began to transform it radically. My destructive addictions were replaced by a hunger and thirst for his Word and for fellowship with Christians. I was able to recognize sin clearly as sin rather than merely make excuses for it as was my previous habit. I can still remember the delicious joy I felt when for the first time black was once more black and white was once more white; the two ceased to pool together as indistinguishable gray.

About a month after entrusting my life to Jesus, God convinced me that his promises are a reality. I heard the report of a Wycliffe [Bible Translators] missionary who served in Nepal. He reported that while he was away, his newly converted language helper was thrown into prison because it is illegal to become a Christian in Nepal. He also reported what this new Christian said at his trial. On the basis of earlier reports which I had heard about this language helper, it instantly became evident that he could never have given such an answer merely on the basis of his own ability. Mark 13:9–11 surged before my eyes[2]—a passage of which I had earlier taken note with only academic interest—and I had no choice but to admit that here was a fulfillment of this promise.

Suddenly I was convinced that God's promises are a reality, that God is a living God, and that he reigns. "For he spoke, and it came to be; he commanded, and it stood firm" (Ps. 33:9). All that I had heard from testimonies in recent months fell into place at that moment. I became aware of what folly it is, given what God is doing today, to maintain that the miracles reported in the New Testament never took place. Suddenly it was clear to me that my teaching was a case of the blind leading the blind. I repented for the way I had misled my students.

About a month after this, alone in my room and quite apart from any input from others around me, I found myself faced with a momentous decision. Would I continue to control the Bible by my intellect, or would I allow my thinking to be transformed by the Holy Spirit? John 3:16 shed light on this decision, for I had recently experienced the truth of this verse. My life now consisted of what God had done for me and for the whole world—he had given his dear Son. I could no longer brush this verse aside as the nonbinding, meaningless theological assertion of a more-or-less gnostic writer.[3] Faith can rest on God's binding promise; speculative theological principles are of merely academic interest.

By God's grace I experienced Jesus as the one whose name is above all names. I was permitted to realize that Jesus *is* God's Son, born of a virgin. He *is* the Messiah and the Son of Man;

---

2. ["You must be on your guard. You will be handed over to the local councils and flogged in the synagogues. On account of me you will stand before governors and kings as witnesses to them. And the gospel must first be preached to all nations. Whenever you are arrested and brought to trial, do not worry beforehand about what to say. Just say whatever is given you at the time, for it is not you speaking, but the Holy Spirit."]

3. [As one might well do if one followed the lead of Linnemann's teacher Rudolf Bultmann; see his *The Gospel of John* (Philadelphia: Westminster, 1971).]

such titles were not merely conferred on him as the result of human deliberation. I recognized, first mentally, but then in a vital, experiential way, that Holy Scripture is inspired.

Not because of human talk but because of the testimony of the Holy Spirit in my heart, I have clear knowledge that my former perverse teaching was sin. At the same time I am happy and thankful that this sin is forgiven me because Jesus bore it on the cross.

That is why I say "No!" to historical-critical theology. I regard everything that I taught and wrote before I entrusted my life to Jesus as refuse. I wish to use this opportunity to mention that I have pitched my two books *Gleichnisse Jesu* . . .[4] and *Studien zur Passionsgeschichte*, along with my contributions to journals, anthologies, and *Festschriften*.[5] Whatever of these writings I had in my possession I threw into the trash with my own hands in 1978. I ask you sincerely to do the same thing with any of them you may have on your own bookshelf.

> Dr. Eta Linnemann
> Professor (retired)
> July 5, 1985

---

4. [This work appears in English translation as *Jesus of the Parables. Introduction and Exposition* (New York: Harper & Row, 1966).]

5. [In addition to her books, Linnemann's earlier publications included: "Überlegungen zur Parabel vom grossen Abendmahl, Lc. 14, 15–24/Mt. 22, 1–14," *ZNW* 51 (1960) 246–55; "Die Verleugnung des Petrus," *ZTK* 63 (1966): 1–32 (in which the historicity of Mark 14:54 and 66–72, is denied); "Der (wiedergefundene) Markusschluss," *ZTK* (1969): 255–87 (in which Linnemann proposes that Mark's original ending consisted of 16:8, then two verses preserved in Matt. 28:16f., and finally Mark 16:15–20); "Tradition und Interpretation in Röm 1, 3f.," *EvT* 31 (1971): 264–75; "Die Hochzeit zu Kana und Dionysus oder das Unzureichende der Kategorien. übertragung und Identifikation zur Erfassung der religionsgeschichtlichen Beziehungen," *NTS* 20 (1974): 408–18.]

Part 1

Christianity and
the Modern University

1

The Anti-Christian Roots
of the University

The university as a phenomenon of Western culture was from the very beginning a pagan institution. "The university in Athens was closed because of its pagan character [in 529 B.C.]."[1] The re-establishment of the university in the High Middle Ages at the end of the twelfth century occurred in conjunction with renewed interest in aspects of pagan culture as the main object of study.

The *corpus juris civiles* (body of civil law) was the object of study around which the first *universitas magistrorum et scholarium* (university of professors and students) gathered in Bologna, Italy. This law code contained regulations enacted in the Christian era, but as a whole it comprised a collection of laws stemming from pre-Christian, pagan times.

The writings of Aristotle—a pagan philosopher—were the objects of study which gave rise to the founding of the second university, this one in Paris.

The reason for the far-reaching autonomy of this new form of institution lay in a spontaneous scientific interest, an intense desire to know and understand for the sake of truth, which was willing to risk conflict to achieve its aims. In Bologna, it was decided without official authorization or sanction to study the legal code of the Roman emperor Justinian which had been virtually disregarded for 500 years and which was nowhere in force. In Paris attention was focused on the natural-philosophical and

1. R. Kottje and B. Moeller, eds., *Ökumenische Kirchengeschichte*, vol. 1, 157.

metaphysical writings, just then available for the first time in Latin translation, of Aristotle, who stood under the suspicion of heresy.[2]

Scholasticism

Scholasticism undertook "to bring the new rational knowledge into agreement with the articles of faith"[3]—an effort which set the tone for all the theological exertions of the High and Late Middle Ages. But it had made a weighty and fateful decision! Instead of bearing in mind that all the treasures of wisdom and knowledge lie hidden in Christ (Col. 2:3), it was assumed that man requires the wordly wisdom of paganism right alongside God's Word in order to make real intellectual progress. God's Word was reduced to just one of two focal points for determining wisdom and knowledge. The Bible came to be regarded as authoritative only in those areas touching on redemption and the Christian life. Aristotle, in contrast, became the source of all valid knowledge of the world, that is, for the realm of natural sciences, social analysis, and so on. From then on, in other words, God's Word was no longer regarded as reliable for these areas of knowledge. Later, Aristotelian philosophy would be replaced by newly developed sciences that hastily blamed the cosmological errors of Aristotle on God's Word.

This initial recourse to the traditions and writings of pagan antiquity led, already in the Middle Ages, to the institutionalizing of the drive for autonomy as part of the formative essence of the university. The Holy Scripture was still authoritative; the attempt was still made to approach the human wisdom of paganism with the intention of bringing "the new rational knowledge into agreement with the articles of faith."[4] Theology was the queen, and philosophy was declared to be her handmaid. But it did not take long for the pagan mentality, which had been taken as handmaid into the newly founded university, to assume sovereign authority. The former queen was, to be sure, accorded a few eye-catching civil rights for a few hundred more years.

2. W. P. Fuchs, "Universität," in *Neues Pädagogisches Lexikon*, edited by Hans-Hermann Groothoff and Martin Stallmann: 1198f.

3. Ibid.

4. Ibid.

Humanism

At the beginning of modern thought stands the frightful decision, which was carried out by the forces of intellectual leadership, to circumvent God's Word and to seek direction instead in
pagan antiquity. Humanism made the decision to make man the
measure of all things. That was a decisive renunciation of God,
even if such humanism usually adopted a thoroughly pious
deportment and constantly mouthed God's Word. What was said
about God no longer sprang from God's revealed Word but
rather from the human spirit, which increasingly distanced itself
from God's Word.

This is already clear in Pico della Mirandola's conception of
the worth of mankind, a conception which held sway in all of
humanism: "God placed man in the middle of the world without
a secure place, without a distinctive identity, without a special
function, while all these things were granted to the rest of his
creatures. Man is created neither earthly nor heavenly; he can
degenerate into a beast, he can ascend to heaven; everything
depends solely and entirely on his will. It is granted to man to
possess what he wishes, to be what he wants."[5]

Let us stop being deceived by pious sounding words! What is
being said here stands in clear contradiction to God's Word. Not
man but Jesus Christ is the center of creation:

> He is the image of the invisible God, the firstborn over all cre-
> ation. For by him all things were created: things in heaven and
> on earth, visible and invisible, whether thrones or powers or
> rulers or authorities; all things were created by him and for him.
> He is before all things, and in him all things hold together. And
> he is the head of the body, the church; he is the beginning and
> the firstborn from among the dead, so that in everything he
> might have the supremacy. For God was pleased to have all his
> fullness dwell in him, and through him to reconcile to himself all
> things, whether things on earth or things in heaven, by making
> peace through his blood, shed on the cross. [Col. 1:15–20]

Pico claims that "everything depends solely and entirely on
his will" and that humanity "can ascend to heaven" are by no
means true. "It does not, therefore, depend on man's desire or
effort, but on God's mercy" (Rom. 9:16). God's Word states:

5. Kurt Dietrich Schmidt, *Kirchengeschichte*, (4th ed., 1963), 264.

"Salvation is found in no one else, for there is no other name under heaven given to men by which we must be saved" (Acts 4:12). Our Lord Jesus said, "No one comes to the father except through me" (John 14:6) and "No one can come to me unless the Father who sent me draws him" (John 6:44).

Whether humanism sees classical antiquity as the absolute standard to which Christianity must conform, as held by Laurentius Valla, or whether it takes up a critical position with respect to both antiquity and Christianity, as Erasmus of Rotterdam—in either case it stands in contradiction to God's revelation. Even in its most positive form, Christianity under humanism's influence degenerates into "an enlightened religion for passing on humanistic civilization's values, reaching its climax in etiquette and morality, in science and culture."[6]

Humanism declines to recognize God and to acknowledge how he has revealed himself in his Word. In humanism the living Christian faith deteriorates to "Christianity," which is, in turn, understood as "religion"—which as such is, of course, comparable to other religions. "Religion becomes one province among the various other areas of culture. And however many independent areas there are, there are that many standards by which religion is measured."[7]

God's Word is no longer the standard in humanism but is, rather, judged by the standard of humanistic culture. In this way culture—the product of the created human spirit—replaced the revelation of God the Creator. Faith in God, the Creator and Redeemer, was perverted into a subdivision of culture and the life of the human spirit. As a consequence man now regarded God's Word as just a product of the activity of this human spirit. To religion is allotted what Schleiermacher would later term a "pious province in the soul" within the boundaries of which it must operate. Violation of these boundaries was from now on severely punished. When the flesh assumes absolute sovereignty, as occurred in this case, it opposes every living manifestation of the Spirit.

For humanism it can be said:

> There is basically only one thing that obligates man, the *veritas* [truth]; but this is always only one, although it takes various

6. Ibid., 269.
7. Ibid., 266.

shapes. "As much as the systems of pagan and Christian thinkers appear to diverge from each other," stated Pico, "they are all basically the offshoots of one and the same truth." The Enlightenment itself hardly relativized all religions in any more radical fashion. And the ethics of Christianity was drawn into this relativizing process.[8]

Humanism, therefore, attributes the status of truth to every product whatsoever of human thought and creativity. The only standard which man still possessed was, thereby, relativized.[9] Man's relativized subjectivity, which by itself is unable to furnish a real foundation for judgments and methods, is given free rein. Now without judgments and methods, there could be no communication within the scientific community. But it must be noted that the systems relied on by science and culture have, under humanistic premises, no real basis, but are grounded in nothing more than arrangements and agreements.

In this approach, everything is ostensibly true and valuable that demonstrates itself to be such on the basis of its inherent quality. In fact, however, nothing can be regarded as true and culturally valuable unless it is acknowledged by the dominant forces which shape science and culture, what we might call the science and culture industry.[10] The methods of science and the systems of evaluation in culture furnish a residence for humanity outside the truth of revelation. But this residence, which we

8. Ibid., 266f.

9. See excursus 2.

10. Regarding the cultural industry, censorship is exercised by cultural currents. This became evident in the controversy regarding the exhibits of the Kasseler "Dokumenta," [an art exhibit that takes place every few years in the German city of Kassel]. Much was excluded which satisfied requirements of quality but did not go along with the current trends. On the other hand, the most inane absurdities were hyped as "art" by the exhibit organizers. [Linnemann cites as examples of "inane absurdities" a one-kilometer-deep hole drilled in the ground in front of the exhibition center under supervision of the late German artist Joseph Beuys. Exhibition officials accepted this as an entry in the show, while excluding high quality but less trendy art works. Linnemann reports that the same artist in another show once displayed a piece consisting of eleven pounds of butter thrown a glob at a time into the upper corner of a room in the Düsseldorf Art Institute. The resulting spectacle was apparently taken seriously as art by some, for a student of Beuys, to whom the late Beuys reportedly gave the piece as a gift, was awarded some $20,000 in damages when overzealous janitorial staff cleaned up what they took to be a mess.] Regarding the scientific industry see chapters 6 and 7.

may liken to a modern Tower of Babel designed to bring the human race together, does not prevent the scattering and fragmentation of human thought and life, but rather causes it. For dissent is built into the system and is an ongoing feature of the science and culture industry.

It is undeniable that agreements are struck which make ongoing operations possible, but how does this occur? Authorities and trendy leaders emerge, by no means on the basis of the quality of their work alone, but based every bit as much on imponderables which have nothing to do with their work.[11] Group dynamics play a decisive role here, and the result is a framework of tradition in the scientific disciplines and in the culture industry. The ostensibly "independent" sciences are steered by their own traditions, and the individual is granted freedom only insofar as that person's work can be integrated into the traditional framework of the discipline.[12]

Genuine freedom of thought exists only where there is truth, and truth is present only in connection with him who is the way, the truth, and the life (John 14:6). There is truth only in Jesus. In humanism truth is replaced by recognition, a prestige wrapped up in the conferring and accepting of honor. This enterprise is, without doubt, subject to manipulation.[13]

The Enlightenment

In comparison to the anti-Christian intellectual stance of humanism, the Enlightenment actually introduces nothing new. It just lays down the conditions for the execution of the humanist agenda.

When Francis Bacon decreed that "every truth [is] found inductively,"[14] he rendered the establishment of man as the measure of all things methodologically feasible. At the same time, the Holy Scripture was excluded as the source of truth.

11. See chapter 9.

12. Discussed further in chapter 7.

13. It would appear to be time to view gifts and endowments; contributions for building, capital, and personnel; federal research grants and other subsidies; as the direct or indirect strengthening of desired trends in culture and science. Who decides what is worthy of further support, and by what criteria are these decisions made?

14. N. L. Geisler, "Das philosophische Vorverständnis der Bibelkritik," in *Bibel und Gemeinde* (1984): 390.

Consistent with his outlook he separated "the realm of reason and science totally from that of faith and religion"[15] and defined faith as *sacrificium intellectus*, the surrender of the attempt to understand.

Hobbes, who likewise made a radical separation between faith and thought, relegated matters of faith "to the unverifiable, paradoxical realm of absurdities and contradictions."[16] He stated, "There is no concept in the human understanding which did not first of all spring, entirely or partially, from the sense organs."[17]

In this way, not only were the foundations of biblical criticism laid—for Hobbes had already initiated them—but the atheistic starting point of the sciences as a whole was likewise fixed. Spinoza, Descartes, Kant—just to name some of many—only stated more precisely what was already laid down in the beginning stages of the Enlightenment.

German Idealism

The ideas which arose in humanism then took on mature form in German idealism. The educational system became even more deeply rooted in the image of man taught by classical antiquity. The Freemason Wilhelm von Humboldt played an especially strategic role in this.[18]

The philosophy of the Enlightenment, which found its crowning achievement in Kant, took form in literature. German authors of the early Romantic period such as Lessing, Schiller, and Goethe remade humanity, so to speak, in the image of the picture they derived from this philosophy. Through "poetic inspiration"[19] their literary characters took on lively and convincing features. They became prototypes of the modern individual; through official sanction and wide distribution of these writings in school curricula, a whole new "model line" of per-

15. Ibid., 391.
16. Ibid., 393.
17. Ibid., 392.
18. See Gottfried Meskemper, *Falsche Propheten unter Dichtern und Denkern* (2d ed., Berneck, 1983).
19. All the figures just cited claimed to be inspired by a spirit outside themselves; Goethe explicitly linked this spirit with demons (see Meskemper, *Falsche Propheten*, 29–33), and in the case of the others we can, judging from the results of their work, hardly avoid suspecting a similar source. It was certainly not the Holy Spirit!

sons was mass-produced as surely as new cars, identical to a designer's prototype, roll off an assembly line. Then, what was absorbed in school by way of vivid conception was, with the inestimably effective assistance of the theatre, transformed into abstract thinking by the university.

Hegel's philosophy took its form in the teaching of history and permeated each and every schoolroom—along with Lessing's thoughts on the *Education of the Human Race* and Herder's *Ideas for a Philosophy of the History of Mankind*. This facilitated the acceptance of Hegel's descendants, Marx and Engels, who in turn paved the way for the Frankfurt school. A scientific historiography arose which first excluded God as an active agent in the historical process by introducing "a god of the philosophers" who conveyed awareness of himself immanently in the course of history. This pseudo-god soon turned out to be superfluous, but he had served to eliminate the possibility of the true God's real and ongoing activity in human history. In this way there came to be a totally atheistic historical "science."

The above remarks must suffice for a sketch of the history of ideas, a sketch which can only throw out a few beams of light. I am quite aware that the presentation of the connections is provisional and that much was passed over. This is due both to time and to personal limitations. Much supplemental material is certainly available in evangelical literature that I have not been able to consult. The reader who is so inclined is encouraged to round out what I have sketched from the wealth of his or her personal knowledge of relevant information. I would of course be thankful for references to such information.[20]

I have intentionally passed over the question of the relationship between the Reformation and Protestant orthodoxy to humanism. Nor have I examined the connection between pietism and the Enlightenment. Much has been written in these areas. As far as the university is concerned, it is in any case humanism and the Enlightenment, not the Reformation and pietism, which have proved to exert long term and one-sided influence.

It has not been my purpose to perform an academic "stocktaking." I want rather to show how this segment of history and

20. I have recently been referred to the study by N. C. van Velzen, which is a considerably more detailed presentation of pertinent aspects of the history of ideas: "Oorsprong en ontwikkeling van het humanisme," *Bijbel en Wetenschap*, 10:79, 4–14.

its consequences appear in the light of God's Word. And I want to issue a long-overdue call for repentance. I am not writing for an academic public but for all who are willing to allow themselves to be admonished by God's Word.

For the purpose of raising the most pertinent questions it is not absolutely necessary to probe more deeply into the history of ideas in the West and their interconnections. This much is established: The die was cast . . .

- after the Middle Ages resorted to pagan philosophy as the means of gaining intellectual orientation;
- after humanism declared man to be the measure of all things;
- after the Enlightenment had decided to acknowledge as truth only that which had been arrived at inductively;
- after the starting premise of Descartes had gained acceptance, according to which the only possibility of verification was through conferring validity to doubt;
- after Lessing, in agreement with Reimarus, had proclaimed the "ugly ditch" between "contingent facts of history" and "eternal truths of reason" and made popular through Nathan the Wise the idea that no one can say what the true faith is;
- after Kant wrote his critique of pure reason and his conception of "Religion within the Bounds of Reason" began to gain acceptance;
- after Goethe's Faust implanted in every cultured person the idea that "our view is barred . . . from seeing spiritual reality" and what—according to the exchange between Faust and Gretchen—one should think of religion;
- after Schleiermacher had drawn the consequences from Kant's criticisms of reason and attempted to ground faith in human religious experience rather than divine revelation;
- after Semler's point of departure in criticism of the Bible, a result of Enlightenment philosophy, began to gain acceptance in biblical exegesis, and
- when an atheistic historiography had established itself.

The elements listed above acquired the status of the binding intellectual starting point among the cultured and became determinative for the university. At first hailed as "man's emancipation from an immaturity for which he himself was guilty"[21] and borne along by a stubborn optimism, after World War I this intellectual starting point came to be understood increasingly as the necessary destiny of the course of human reflection. One way or another, this starting point was and continues to be seen as necessary and inescapable, and as a result vehemently advocated—with the assistance of influence, financial resources, and political might.

In the university, which from the start was an anti-Christian institution, there was soon no place for thinking which based itself consistently on God's revelation in his Word.[22]

The Age of Technology

Technical education found itself, to be sure, so much in opposition to the educational ideal of the Humboldt universities[23] that the founding of some alternate education centers became necessary. However, the intellectual starting point of technology was based every bit as much on the Enlightenment as was the humanist-idealist concept of education. In both cases God was methodologically excluded from the outset, even by researchers whose personal piety was unquestioned. In this way technology and education were finally able to come to an agreement, once

21. Immanuel Kant, *Was ist Aufklärung?* (1784).

22. The accusation that pietism abandoned the field of academic teaching is unjustified, for it gives rise to the false impression that pietism could relate to academic theology however it wished, and that it is to blame for the result of the course it followed. This position overlooks the fact that there was no place in the university for theology loyal to the Bible once humanism's and the Enlightenment's atheistic outlooks became the normative starting point among the cultured and the framework within which academic theology was forced to develop.

23. [Wilhelm von Humboldt (1767–1835), noted statesman, humanist, and linguist, was chief intellectual architect of the University of Berlin, which he helped found about 1810. He insisted that the mission of the university was this alone: "Seek learning for its own sake, having no regard for anything else." German universities founded on the Berlin model, which became a prototype, were accordingly quite out of sympathy with the concept of university education as technical research leading to professional education. See Wilhelm Humboldt, "Higher Learning in Berlin," in *Great Ideas Today*, edited by R. M. Hutchins and M. J. Adler (Chicago: Encyclopedia Britannica, 1969): 350–55.]

the success of technology could no longer be overlooked. The success of the atheistic intellectual starting point in technology appeared to give it ultimate confirmation. And this apparent confirmation stigmatized every objection as folly.

Is it possible to oppose thinking that produces the machines that we use daily, that organizes the transportation systems, that furnishes central heat and electric current without which modern life appears to be impossible?

It is already hammered into every school-age child today that it is not possible to oppose modern thought, that "today we no longer live in the Middle Ages, thank goodness!" and that even "alternative lifestyles" are possible only in the shadow of technical development.

Every student who entrusts himself to the university must accept the yoke of the atheistic intellectual starting point as an inescapable necessity. This is a yoke which bends the bearer cruelly, and which is placed on the student apart from conscious choice, by means of the completion of the course of study in a major field—a field dominated by the atheistic starting point. Even Christians who attend the university come under this yoke. They are permitted, to be sure, to have their faith in their private lives by those around them who may view that faith favorably, or derisively, or perhaps even share its convictions. But they are forbidden to retain the living God and his Son Jesus Christ in their academic thinking, or to grant him any material function therein.[24] So they retain Jesus in their feelings, but they deny him daily in their thinking, because this thinking follows atheistic, anti-Christian principles.[25]

The monopolistic character of atheistically based centers of education results in the whole of technical achievements being credited to the account of atheistic "scientific" thought. People behave as did Israel when its people thought they were receiving wool and flax, grain and wine from the Baals, instead of

24. See Lutz von Padberg, "Gegen die Aufspaltung von Glauben und Denken," *Idea Dokumentation* 33 (1985); Ranald Macauley, "Das christliche Denken," *factum* (May 1985). See also excursus 2.

25. For this reason we need academic institutions where thought in all disciplines can get right to work on the foundation of God's Word, instead of—at best—exhausting itself in trying to refute prevalent errors. It is essential that we break out of the traditional connections of individual disciplines as quarries from which we may, with utmost caution, salvage usable material. In short, we need colleges that will give the Bible its rightful place!

thanking its Creator for these things (Hos. 2:1–13). But people do not own up to the very real negative effects of science which inevitably accompany the positive findings. They do not face up to the consequences of the law of sin which is still in effect when one takes part in scientific exchange.

Everywhere this thinking, rooted in godlessness, bears fruit today we can see that the fruit is bitter. In all areas of life man is trying to take control of his own ship. Meanwhile the ship is out of control, and many live in a state of helpless perplexity.

In spite of all the progress that medicine has made it has not done away with sickness. True, a few diseases appear to be conquered, and others are on the verge of losing the terror they formerly held. But new ones are cropping up and spreading. Seen as a whole, humanity is hardly healthier, only more dependent on physicians and medicine. Where child and infant mortality had been conquered, now abortion and sterilization take place in assembly-line fashion. Hardly one helpful prescription drug does not cause a number of negative side effects.

Technical progress brings with it destruction of the environment to an extent previously unknown in human history. Effort is centered on discovering means of destruction (atomic, biological, and chemical weapons) for the purpose of annihilating persons and whole nations. Without our vaunted technical progress this would have been unimaginable. A large number of new chemical weapons lie in arsenals for eventual use. To date only the few whose occupations require it even know of some of these.

In spite of all developments in biology and agricultural sciences, the nourishment of mankind is not ensured. Now that humanity, through its interference, has destroyed the biological balance, we must attempt to counteract the effects, often using poisons that bring about damaging effects of their own. The possibility of genetic engineering, one of the results of progress in research, has its apparent advantages in the area of cattle-breeding, but it also turns out to have corrupting potential for mankind. Sociology, the youngest of the sciences, while it is billed as a means of addressing and solving social ills, has been and is being widely used to destroy natural social ties.

In place of the projected "maturity" of the thinking person we see modern society patronized by the tyranny of experts. Even in the most basic areas, the life of the "liberated" modern person is allowed to be dictated by experts who on the basis of their "expertise" (which they have often not shown to be valid even in their own personal lives) have become "authorities." In place of the *one* Book of God's wisdom, by which modern man does not wish to be instructed, we have the many mutually contradictory books that claim validity for themselves on the basis of being "scientific."

"Science-based" public sex education patronizes and corrupts sexual behavior by destroying the natural sense of shame.

Experts are adduced to explain how many children one is able to afford ("Two are plenty!"), and experts lay claim to the authority to decide how these children ought to be brought up. The poor parents and society harvest the bitter fruits of this upbringing, while the experts, in the meantime, have long since progressed to new theories of child-rearing.

"Scientifically-assured" statistics and public-opinion polls which the experts produce in abundance determine the modern lifestyle, a lifestyle which can often only be addressed in terms of addictive behavior steered by the pleasure principle.

Taken together, all this is leading to an unprecedented worldwide homogenizaton of thought and behavior. Alternative behavior is discouraged; there is pressure to conform to the emerging societal norms. Of man's projected and vaunted "maturity" there is no trace!

"Sapere aude! Have the courage to rely on your own understanding!" was the motto of the Enlightenment. That is what Kant declared in his 1784 publication, *What Is Enlightenment? Sapere aude!* was already implicitly propagated by humanism. *Sapere aude!*—that was the resolution to accept revelation no longer but to replace it with the arbitrary authority of reason. *Sapere aude!*—that was the decision made by "the godlessness and wickedness of men who suppress the truth by their wickedness" (Rom. 1:18).

God answered this decision with judgment:

> The wrath of God is being revealed from heaven against all the godlessness and wickedness of men who suppress the truth by their wickedness, since what may be known about God is plain to them, because God has made it plain to them. For since the creation of the world God's invisible qualities—his eternal power and divine nature—have been clearly seen, being understood from what has been made, so that men are without excuse.
>
> For although they knew God, they neither glorified him as God nor gave thanks to him, but their thinking became futile and

their foolish hearts were darkened. Although they claimed to be
wise, they became fools. . . .[Rom. 1:18–22]

What applies to the pagan who can only apprehend God's
revelation in the creation applies to a far greater degree for him
who has been made aware of God's revelation in his Son!
"Although they claimed to be wise, they became fools!" The history of the last five hundred years in all its facets—political history as well as intellectual, the history of technology as well as
theology—offers a clear testimony to the wrath to which God
has delivered us.

In view of the frightful wickedness we have committed, this
history is also a witness to God's abounding grace and long-
suffering patience. It is "because of the LORD's great love we are
not consumed" (Lam. 3:22).

The current state of affairs is truly deplorable. What a frightful (but respectable-appearing) godlessness we have allowed
ourselves to be sucked into. For over five hundred years now we
have bowed down to a culture and science which were anti-
Christian from the start. We have allowed ourselves to be convinced that thinking and creativity are possible only within this
framework.[26] In this way we have trampled underfoot the gift of
our Father in heaven, his beloved Son, in whom he has granted
us all the riches of wisdom and knowledge (see Col. 2:3).

Decade after decade, century after century, Christianity has
accepted this sacrilege and become ever more deeply implicated
in it. What kindness, patience, and long-suffering has God
shown us: At the same time that the bright light of the gospel
began to beam forth once more, the civilization which glimpsed
its rays turned aside to godlessness—and God put up with
humans and sustained them with his love through the ensuing
centuries! How great is the completed work of Golgotha, whose
streams of blessing flow out even over recent centuries!

Nevertheless: "Today, if you hear his voice, do not harden
your hearts" (Ps. 95:7–8). Let us finally return to the One who
created us. Apart from the saving work God carried out when
he gave his Son for our sin on the cross of Golgotha, he would
have to consign us to eternal separation from God and the
agony of the sea of fire, just on the basis of our participation in
the sacrilege of such godlessness. And that is just what he will
do, if we do not take refuge in Jesus as our Savior.

26. See Note 25.

2

Pertinent Questions Concerning the University

The long time span during which an atheistic, anti-Christian culture and science has spread and won worldwide influence in the "Christian West" has made us indifferent to this monstrosity. It is difficult for us to gain a critical perspective on something which has been established for centuries and seems self-evident. It is difficult to recognize that the history of ideas in the West, encompassing more than five hundred years, is a sinful blunder. We view it, along with its international impact, as a given state of affairs—in keeping with a modern intellectual dogma that what we identify as facts inherently possess normative power for our thought. What *does* exist is confused with and identified as what *should* exist. The factual takes on more weight than the normative and, in fact, becomes normative.

In addition, we are so marked by these cultural and educational forces that we can be freed only by the grace of our Father in heaven, the blood of our Savior Jesus Christ, and the cleansing water of God's Word. We consider attainment of a modern education to be an asset, for it has enabled us to reach the point at which we stand. We have accepted the conventional wisdom that thought and creativity are possible only within this framework.

Even if one is willing to listen, questions arise about the previous chapter's assertions. These questions are not easily dispelled.

Is This Historical Outline Accurate?

Is the short outline of the modern history of ideas not a black-white sketch which fails to do justice to reality?

37

True, neither humanism nor the early Enlightenment consciously implemented a break from the Christian faith. There
was at most an awareness of a conscious stand against church
teaching. Even idealism was by no means a total repudiation of
Christianity. Thus, we may speak of persons being un-Christian
without being consciously anti-Christian.[1] One can find
Christian nomenclature in philosophies ranging from Pico della
Mirandola, Bacon, Hobbes, and Descartes, to Kant, Goethe, and
Hegel. The entire tenor of society was still Christian. Raw atheism was certainly not permitted to raise its ugly head. Even
Lessing bowed to social pressure, though his writings insinuate
that he would have preferred to act differently. Semler directly
stated that his ideas were not for the people but only for the
intelligentsia, at that time a very small group indeed.

We are dealing here with a gradual process of infiltration. The
anti-Christian nature of this view is revealed primarily in its
contradiction of God's Word. It is anti-Christian and atheistic in
that it neglects God, the Father of our Lord Jesus Christ, even as
it piously mouths the word *God*. Its god is not the One who
revealed himself in his Word, but rather the god of the philosophers, to whom is ascribed that which the human spirit dreams
up. Well into the nineteenth century this thinking was generally
quite pious, though this piety surged up less and less frequently.
The rebellious human nature which Paul calls "flesh" (Greek
sarx; see Rom 8:5–8) came to power, presenting itself first as
pious "flesh."

Second, this view's anti-Christian nature becomes evident in
that the study of the Bible and nature methodologically disregards God. God's Word as the source of all knowledge is shoved
aside.

Thought in the West was de-Christianized somewhat like a
caterpillar is devoured from the inside after the ichneumon fly
has laid its eggs; the eggs laid in the caterpillar hatch into larvae,
which in turn develop to feed on their host. The outer form of
the caterpillar remains undamaged for some time until it too is
finally destroyed.

One could also compare the process to the way a frame

---

1. With respect to humanism see van Velzen, "Oorsprung en ontwikkeling
van het humanisme." On the Enlightenment see N. L. Geisler, "Philosophical
Presuppositions of Biblical Inerrancy," in N. L. Geisler, ed., *Inerrancy*, (Grand
Rapids: Zondervan, 1983), esp. 312–24.

house is destroyed by termites. The supporting timbers are covertly attacked, and when they are fully weakened, the building collapses.

Similarly we are seeing the results in modern thought of what has been going on undercover for a long time. The false impression is created that the Christian faith has come to an end. What has happened is that a stream of ideology, which was anti-Christian from the start, has finally run its course. This ideology was at first intermixed with the Christian faith; but in the course of its refinement it rejected the Christian faith as essentially incompatible.

The illusion that the Christian faith is obsolete arose solely because too many Christians identified their faith with this ideology that has ended. They did not recognize the anti-Christian character it possessed from the beginning. The Christian faith, meanwhile, remained protected by God's grace—there have always been the "seven thousand" who did not bow the knee to Baal (Rom. 11:4–5). These were, nevertheless, often persons whom Paul would describe as "not many . . . wise by human standards; not many . . . influential; not many . . . of noble birth" (1 Cor. 1:26). In addition, the Christian faith was barred from development in the academic centers of learning where the atheistically conceived notion of science held monopolistic sway. Access to this world was restricted in that few could enter it without sacrificing their faith.

The contemporary situation was quite muddled due to the syncretistic mixing of Christianity with notions alien to it, but we can now by God's grace see it clearly. Let us use this hour of grace to renounce this sinful syncretism and in the name of Jesus make a new beginning. "Break up your unplowed ground and do not sow among thorns" (Jer. 4:3).

Are We Not to Stay in the World?

Is the result of chapter 1 not irrelevant, since it is obvious that the university, too, is "the world"? After all, Jesus did not request that we be taken out of the world, but rather that we be preserved in it (John 17:15).

Initially this argument seems reasonable, yet one must make a crucial distinction. If I buy groceries in the world, what I buy and eat is simply consumed and digested; it does not come in contact with my thinking. If I buy shoes from an atheist or pagan, the shoes only touch my feet, not the inner person. If I work on the assembly line in a factory, I might have to listen to vulgar or blasphemous talk by those around me, but I am not compelled to absorb this profanity into my mind. If I sit at a desk in a management post, I might have to give attention to laws and regulations, but these restrictions do not alter me personally. The university, in contrast, is where thinking is altered and brought into line with the world.

Ever since Enlightenment society rejected the reality of the Fall (Gen. 3), along with resulting human depravity and need for redemption, humanity has tried to portray thinking as a neutral, objective, and effective capacity. Everything that appears to conform to the laws of logic is automatically correct and reliable, insofar as it restricts itself monistically to what is visible and immanent. This conviction of neutrality, objectivity, and the universality of scientific thought is championed in the university, where it is assumed that true "thinking" must be "scientifically based," and so limited to these monistic self-restrictions. In other words, the sciences which can be studied in the university, each in their respective domains, lay a claim to exclusive validity for human thought.

Through this stridently advocated claim to exclusive validity, students wanting to learn to think are drawn into the world-wide process of secularization. They are, as already suggested, brought into line with the world. Yet God's Word admonishes us: "Do not conform any longer to the pattern of this world, but be transformed by the renewing of your mind. Then you will be able to test and approve what God's will is—his good, pleasing, and perfect will" (Rom. 12:2). What we absorb through our thinking forms the kind of person we become. The saying, "Tell me who you run around with, and I'll tell you what kind of person you are" recognizes this assumption. Is it possible for me to spend eight or nine hours a day in modes of thought based on atheistic, anti-Christian premises without being profoundly swayed?

Scientific thought surely has the appearance of neutrality. It methodologically excludes God and thereby assures itself that he has nothing to do with the construction of machines, the development of chemicals that protect plants from disease, the interpretation of poetry, or the determination of historical dates. Yet it is precisely this claim of neutrality, this methodological exclusion of God, that stands in contradiction to God's Word. This very approach is atheistic and anti-Christian.

If I adopt this approach, I reduce God to a peripheral phenomenon, whether or not this is my intention. I dismiss large portions of his Word daily without being aware of it and am soon left with a very small god, a god relevant only to my private life, a god who will not bear me up when life's serious demands press me down. But this minimalization is not because God is somehow limited; it is rather because of the way I confine the scope of God's reign. We reap what we sow (Gal. 6:7), and this truth also applies to our intellectual life.

Christian research, in contrast, strives to depend on God in the selection of the object of study, in the means adopted for study, and in the motives for study. It attempts to rely on God at every step. Such research cannot "be autonomous and uninhibitedly subjective; it must rather find its point of reference and confirmation directly or indirectly in the Scripture."[2] The world cannot agree with this reliance, but it can share in the fruits of such labor.

What about the Christians in Universities?

Some may raise another objection to the previous chapter: Not everyone who did or does teach and study in the institutions described is godless. Among them there were and are many "wise and noble". In fact, many were and are children of God who are shining witnesses for Jesus. Does not what you have said about the university amount to judging people who have labored there according to the best of their knowledge with a clean conscience and with utmost exertion? Is it not arrogant to batter them in this fashion?

I respond that it is *not* my intention to batter anyone. God's Word admonishes us, "Therefore judge nothing before the appointed time; wait till the Lord comes. He will bring to light what is hidden in darkness and will expose the motives of men's hearts. At that time each will receive his praise from God" (1 Cor. 4:5).

Neither am I trying to pressure children of God nor blame them for their current stations. As long as the university maintains its monopoly, there is every likelihood that individual chil-

2. "Das christliche Denken," 8.

dren of God will find their place there under his leadership. Each is called to serious self-examination before the Lord, for "Who are you to judge someone else's servant? To his own master he stands or falls" (Rom. 14:4a). My critique applies to the university institution and the institutionalization of the science and culture industries. The critique is not directed toward individual persons but toward a system. We must clarify our relationship to this system; we need to examine ourselves. Do we wish to continue to identify with it, exposing ourselves to its influence as we have in the past? God's Word speaks clearly on this matter: "Do not be yoked together with unbelievers. For what do righteousness and wickedness have in common? Or what fellowship can light have with darkness? What harmony is there between Christ and Belial? What does a believer have in common with an unbeliever?" (2 Cor. 6:14–15).

Or to quote a recent writer:

> The false human conceptual structures, the "hollow and deceptive philosophy, which depends on human tradition" (Col. 2:8) and "every pretension that sets itself up against the knowledge of God" (2 Cor. 10:5), are like dangerous pollution of the water supply that services our homes. They delude and destroy everywhere, especially in our own culture, which has traded its former foundation for that of humanism and materialism. The media and the academic world have all, in one form or another, united themselves with humanistic thinking, so that it would be justified to affix "humanistic" to the title of every scientific discipline. Should the members of these disciplines who know they are obligated to the Bible just sit there and abandon the field without a struggle?[3]

Has Not Much Scientific Work Been Useful?

A fourth cluster of responses to the previous chapter might be along this line: Surely not everything that has resulted from the scientific work of recent centuries is bad. Would you not admit that much of it should be seen as helpful?

I agree fully. We spoke earlier of the two faces or sides of science. God in his faithfulness, patience, and mercy has continued to grant blessings; he has by his grace granted much that is beneficial and helpful during these centuries of sinful error. But,

---

3. Ibid., 9.

due to such sinful error, the good has also been corrupted into that which is damaging and destructive. It would presumably be worthwhile to trace the course of sin, grace, and judgment in the individual scientific disciplines, but that is not my task. I will make a few exploratory remarks on this topic in excursus 2.

What should we do now? Can we do anything at all, or must we simply lament the centuries of error and purify ourselves spiritually? Can we conjure up new centers of learning? What shape would they take? These are questions which will occupy our attention in chapter 4.

"But is it really conceivable that God, our Lord, the Almighty who reigns, has looked on and permitted a centuries-long course of error to develop in this way? Can we seriously entertain the notion that he has chosen not to intervene as generation after generation have served as misled misleaders? Do we not rather have to regard what has been and is as what was and is supposed to be?" God's Word gives us the answer to these questions, which we explore in chapter 3.

3

Ancient Israel and the Modern West

God's Word, which was written for our instruction, does not leave us guessing with respect to the question posed at the end of chapter 2. It gives us knowledge and insight into the way things really are.

A Parallel in the History of Israel

The monstrous developments which we have traced in the course of the history of ideas in the so-called Christian West have a frightening parallel in the history of the people of Israel, in the setting up of the golden calves in Bethel and Dan. Israel had split into two kingdoms, in the south Judah and Benjamin, and in the north the other ten tribes. This division was God's response to Solomon's sin. King Solomon had provoked God by allowing temples to be erected for the false gods of his foreign wives. This compounded the error he had already committed in sealing these marriages for political purposes in defiance of God's wishes. God himself had foretold his judgment to Solomon; it would take place following his death. While Solomon was still alive, the prophet Ahijah informed Jeroboam that he would become king of the ten tribes.

Jeroboam became king of the northern kingdom by God's grace and according to God's will, and the selfsame Jeroboam fell away from God and took the people with whom he was entrusted down with him:

> Jeroboam thought to himself, "The kingdom will now likely revert to the house of David. If these people go up to offer sacrifices at the temple of the LORD in Jerusalem, they will again give their allegiance to their lord, Rehoboam king of Judah. They will kill me and return to King Rehoboam."

> After seeking advice, the king made two golden calves. He said to the people, "It is too much for you to go up to Jerusalem. Here are your gods, O Israel, who brought you up out of Egypt." One he set up in Bethel, and the other in Dan. And this thing became a sin; the people went even as far as Dan to worship the one there.
>
> Jeroboam built shrines on high places and appointed priests from all sorts of people, even though they were not Levites. . . . On the fifteenth day of the eighth month, a month of his own choosing, he offered sacrifices on the altar he had built at Bethel. So he instituted the festival for the Israelites and went up to the altar to make offerings. [1 Kings 12:26–31, 33]

Although a prophet from Judah spoke to him at the altar in Bethel and made God's judgment known by various signs, "Jeroboam did not change his evil ways, but once more appointed priests for the high places from all sorts of people. Anyone who wanted to become a priest he consecrated for the high places" (1 Kings 13:33).

With the installation of the "golden calves" in Israel for political reasons, the sin of apostasy was institutionalized. The inspiration for this was drawn from outside Israel, where the bull was regarded as the symbol of divine power. This sin already had a tradition: Aaron had previously cast an image of a calf. Sin sets precedents and (mis)leads to imitation. The judgment of Aaron's sin, and that of the children of Israel with him at the foot of Sinai, had not been that many centuries ago. Had not Moses intervened, the entire people would have been annihilated! Even so, Moses set in motion a punishment for the sin in which 3000 men lost their lives.

This sin was plainly stated to be sin. This was common knowledge up through the time of Jeroboam, but how quickly it was forgotten! A few centuries prior to Jeroboam, the Levites sided with Moses when Aaron sought to institute idol worship. By Jeroboam's time the prophet from Judah who confronted him at the altar in Bethel, where the apostasy had been institutionalized, found no one who openly sided with him. Had the people of Israel already been corrupted by letting Solomon's sin go by without confronting him? Had the people let the brilliance which Solomon brought to Israel blind them? Were people content just to enjoy the prosperity Solomon's rule ushered in? "The people of Judah and Israel were as numerous as the sand on the seashore; they ate, they drank and they were happy. And Solomon ruled over all the kingdoms from the River to the land of the Philistines, as far as the border of Egypt. These countries brought tribute and were Solomon's subjects all his life" (1 Kings 4:20–21).

Jeroboam made use of a lie: "Here are your gods, O Israel, who brought you up out of Egypt." He foisted strange gods on Israel. He misled the people. The simple folk would hardly have detected it; they took the lying words of the king at face value. They failed to see through his deception. Many a brave and sincere-hearted Israelite went on to make sacrifice at Bethel or Dan without realizing that sacrificial offerings at these sites were an abomination to the Lord!

Those who were in a position to know better—and there must have been some in Israel—held their peace. None of them opened their mouths and stood up for God's honor. Everyone consented—due to fear? Due to laziness? Due to apathy? There was not one person who sought God, not even one (see Rom. 3:11–18). How horrid is the character even of the old prophet (1 Kings 13)! At the cost of the younger prophet's life, for whose death he was largely responsible, he confirmed that the younger prophet's message was genuine. But the call for repentance went no farther. What he knew remained a useless piece of hidden knowledge for him and his sons and did not result in a call for repentance which might have kindled widespread willingness to make a radical turnabout.

Jeroboam assumed the role of the trustworthy ruler. He affected to be concerned for the people, when in fact his concern was only for his own sovereignty ("It is too much for you to go up to Jerusalem."). He used the fleshly tendency to laziness for his own gain. In every respect he was willing to support the inclinations of the flesh; in the holy sanctuaries every religiously gilded sinful tendency was indulged, and everyone who had the desire to appear in such a role was ordained a priest. The sinful and "pious" flesh was encouraged to develop without hindrance.

Developments in the West since the Middle Ages

The biblical pattern speaks for itself, but I would like to call special attention to several observations which characterize developments since the Middle Ages (see chapter 1) and which are paralleled in the Old Testament accounts just considered:

First, there were only a few—perhaps at first only one—who consciously made the decision not to regard God's Word as normative any longer. Their social position lent weight to this decision; this implies that the people were already to some degree secularized and for that reason regarded the person instead of God. One person, or the tiny majority, became the instigator of a trend.

Second, the ever-present tendency of the flesh and of sin was strengthened and given legitimacy by the leadership it followed. It was encouraged to develop without hindrance. The standard became life as seems right to fleshly tendencies rather than life appropriate to the Spirit. The flesh in its hostility to God was established and institutionalized.

Third, since the fleshly life was declared to be "normal," a seductive undertow was set in motion. It was granted to each individual to make out of himself whatever he could. What at first was made possible by official permission and assistance soon became an expected right, as when in the time of Jeroboam unqualified persons became priests. Each could do what he wished according to the measure of ability and means at his disposal. The question of what God had in mind was no longer relevant. Man decided his life goals autonomously, without consulting God. Anyone who did not conform to this pattern came under increasing pressure.

Fourth, the tendency was guided by the interest of those in power. First it was the princes who craved the prestige that a university in their territory would bring and who had high hopes of benefiting from one. Today national prestige continues to play a role, although economic interests exert more power; they have a hand in determining the content of curriculum. This is seen in the type of mathematics instruction that is introduced already at the primary-school level. In the same vein, everything is calculated to inculcate a humanistic worldview and a "tolerance" which permits each his own desire and lets each be blessed however he sees fit.

> "Was nicht verboten ist, ist erlaubt.
> Fragt hier keiner, was einer glaubt."[1]

This is a tolerance that is militant against everyone who does not permit himself to be pressed into the mold which is desirable for the citizen of the future one-world empire.

Fifth, the trend procures for itself an institutional monopoly and becomes a conditioning factor. What this monopoly regards as "factual" comes to have normative force.[2] In circular fashion the same monopoly gives an alibi to the godless trend by the participation of the many who promote it and thereby create the aura of a legitimate institution. They do so with the best intentions because they do not know any better and because they apparently have no other option.

Sixth, the one who commits himself to this institution no longer sees it from God's point of view. His perception of God takes on a severely refracted quality.

Seventh, God's view of this institution is that it participates in sin.

---

1. From Schiller's "Wallensteins Lager", lines 318–19:
"Whatever is not forbidden is permissible.
No one here inquires what anyone believes."
2. The modern dogma referred to above (p. 37): What we identify as facts possess, in and of themselves, normative power within our thought. What does exist is confused with—indeed identified as—what should exist. The "factual" takes on more weight than the "normative" and in fact becomes normative.

4

Christian Education
at the University Level

An academic education that is Christian in design—not only in name but in authentic obedience to our Lord and Savior Jesus Christ—can be established only by conscious dissociation from the modern European university and its history, including its historical emanations as these have taken form in America, Africa, and Asia. That also means dissociation from the practice of institutions in which the anti-Christian intellectual starting point is checked only somewhat by a basically evangelical outlook.

It is not enough that teachers and students be Christians and begin their activities with prayer. The *content* of the activities must be fundamentally transformed from the ground up. Entire areas of intellectual inquiry must be grounded in God's Word. "The Bible furnishes the essential framework for intellectual inquiry. Without this framework every science is a foolish enterprise."[1]

The enterprise of making available university-level education centers that are loyal to the Bible will of course encounter critical objections. Even sympathetic observers will express misgivings such as "Is that really a manageable goal?" or "What would

1. Lutz von Padberg, remark in connection with his paper "Gegen die Aufspaltung von Glauben und Denken," presented at the Theological Meeting of the Conference for Confessing Churches, 2–4 October 1985, Hemer, West Germany. See *Idea-Dokumentation* 33 (1985). [Von Padberg explains this statement more systematically in his *Die Bibel—Grundlage für Glauben, Denken und Erkennen: Prolegomena zu einer biblischen Erkenntnislehre* (*The Bible—Foundation for Believing, Thinking, and Knowing: Prolegomena to a Biblical Epistemology*)(Neuhausen-Stuttgart: Hänssler, 1986).]

such a thing, if really necessary, look like?" We now take up these and other objections and queries.

Objections to a Christian Education

The first objection is sure to come with reference to the inevitability of that which has resulted from past historical developments. We are sure to be charged with making the useless attempt to return to the Middle Ages. A return to the Middle Ages, however, would not be enough for us, because the theology of the Middle Ages, as we have already seen, set the pagan philosophy of Aristotle as a second source of knowledge on the same level as Scripture. This is not to mention the influence of neo-Platonism, which had already made its presence felt in the early Middle Ages.

It will be stated to us that it is impossible to turn back the wheel of history, that we will therefore have to put up with the conditions that we find today. Two things may be said to this:

First, this kind of talk is rooted in pure deception since it personifies and ascribes power to history. That power which is inherent to God—because he reigns and steers the destinies of peoples—is wrested from him and given to history, which is assumed to govern like an impersonal *It*. The oft-invoked *wheel of history* appears to be a modification of the *wheel of rebirth*, which is a familiar concept in Hindu and Buddhist religion.

Second, it is by no means our intention to go back or to set ourselves against historical development. We want, rather, to turn back to the living God, our Creator and the Father of our Lord and Savior Jesus Christ. We want to enter into his light in the entire sphere of thought, including education, culture, and science, so that he will forgive and instruct us. He made the sure promise that he will give wisdom to him who asks him for it (James 1:5). He will certainly not deny us the grace to make a new beginning.

The second objection is that, due to the high costs, there is simply no way to pay for the founding of university-level education centers that are loyal to the Bible, centers that would impart education along the entire range of academic disciplines and would carry out the research essential to this. The project is dismissed as unrealistic due to the assumption that it is impossible to raise the necessary funds for the construction and equipping of such centers. Nor could one raise the immense sums necessary for research. To this may be said:

A Christian university worthy of the name would place itself under God's leadership with respect to the question of what it should investigate. This would obviate dabbling in many expensive areas that were started in opposition to God's will and contribute solely to the glorification of man. The underlying dynamic of the university to this point in its history is *competition*. This has given rise to a number of similar university establishments and institutes. Colleges loyal to the Bible would have no need of this duplication of services. Christian investigation of creation takes its basic starting point from God's Word. This obviates much groping in the dark which might result in whole series of expensive experiments. Christian scholarship is—to the extent that scholars truly seek God's honor—led by God's Spirit. He can lead directly to efficient and money-saving means of investigation. To put it succinctly, the objection assumes as a given the current conditions of today's universities and does not take account of the special factors which might affect a college loyal to the Bible.

In addition, one must consider that all resources come from our Creator's hand. He will certainly not deny his blessing to an undertaking which began with persons turning to him with the determination that they will no longer be party to their past sins. Everything here is really a matter of God's blessing. One can already see quite sufficiently from the Christian institutions that have previously come into existence (Christian primary and secondary schools, study centers, and colleges) how wondrously our Father in heaven supports those who seek his ways. Truly, he does not lack means.

One further objection is sure to be raised: There is a total dearth of the personnel required for the establishment of colleges doing university-level work who are loyal to the Bible and who could satisfactorily cover entire disciplines. On the contrary, I perceive with wonder and gratitude to God that our Father in heaven has already prepared persons in the various disciplines. He has assembled many for just such a venture who have already been addressing themselves expressly to the cluster of questions I am raising. Truly, God has preserved within entire scientific disciplines one or more of the "seven thousand . . . whose knees have not bowed down to Baal" (1 Kings 19:18).

Even if at first it is not possible to assemble the needed teachers for a single college loyal to the Bible, the process of multiplication of like-minded thinkers would at least be set in motion. Teachers with suitable academic credentials would be equipped for subsequent colleges loyal to the Bible. In addition, some dissemination of information is possible even at the beginning stages using multi-media aids.[2]

The education center that is loyal to the Bible does not have to leap into existence in one fell swoop. It is possible to initiate the envisioned educational programs through preliminary measures, such as an introductory year of study prior to university elsewhere. This would give impetus to teachers and would furnish them opportunity to think through their areas of expertise based on God's Word.

Making Education Christian

Render a Service to the Body of Christ.

The education center that is loyal to the Bible should understand itself as rendering service within the body of Christ. The work and life both of those who study and those who teach should be determined by the fundamental principle of discipleship. This involves:

- dedicated listening to God's Word (loyalty to the Bible and daily quiet time with it);
- being a doer of the Word (imitating Christ, walking in the light, and sanctification);
- being a witness for Jesus;
- being willing to repent;
- being willing to serve;
- participation in corporate Christian life (accountability to others in the fellowship, giving and taking correction, brotherly encouragement and admonition, along with interceding and being interceded for);
- willingness to serve under someone else's direction;

2. N. C. van Velzen, "Christelijk Hoger Onderwijs Nieuwe Stijl. Nota ter Voorbereidng van een Internationale Christelijke Universiteit/ICU," 1982.

- leading a life under God's direction;
- waiting in God's presence.

It is to be assumed that teachers will exhibit these qualities according to personal levels of spiritual maturity. Regarding the students, the education center that is loyal to the Bible participates in the commission Jesus gave: "Therefore go and make disciples of all nations . . . teaching them to obey everything I have commanded you . . ." (Matt. 28:19–20).

Being a disciple of Jesus in the academic setting cannot be learned merely *prior to* the educational experience but must be learned *as part of* the education. For this reason, such an institution cannot merely serve the interests of professional competence. It must also keep before it the goal of helping students grow in emulating Jesus. Accordingly, Christian fellowship in which there is corporate accountability in everyday life is an unconditional necessity, at least for two years, or still better for three. One year is rather too short to have the impact needed.

Place God's Word in the Center

Since God's Word is the foundation of the entire education, all students, regardless of speciality, should receive a good grounding in the Bible. This includes information about the Bible as well as a systematic understanding of what the Bible teaches. The systematic presentation of what the Bible teaches should cover such areas as God's overall plan of salvation, a thorough grasp of fundamental biblical concepts, and fundamentals of a biblical hermeneutic.

Along with information about the Bible as well as a systematic understanding of what the Bible teaches, students should be taught the biblical bases for all areas of study. This should be required for all students, with specialized studies in students' own individual disciplines.

Make Neither Theology Nor Philosophy Foundational

I recommend refraining from including theology as a foundational subject. The very concept of *theology* has, in my opinion, too much the connotation of humanly conceived systems. This could very easily point students in the wrong direction. They should not be instructed in theoretical theological constructs; they should, rather, become more deeply and broadly rooted and grounded in God's Word, which furnishes the cognitive framework for work in the individual disciplines.

Philosophy likewise seems to me problematic as a foundational subject, even when one attempts to give it a new content by making it a Christian theory of science. In the long run the basic tendency of this discipline in its original conception will show its true colors.

Is there any legitimate place at all for philosophy in the education center that is loyal to the Bible? Philosophy as taught in the university has a number of aspects. The emphasis lies on the *history* of philosophy—the sorting, assessing, and accurate passing on of the various philosophical systems. Less stress is placed on new systems of philosophy which arise from this history, either as the applications of the overall vision of the discipline or (rarely) as the result of some genuinely original new starting point. Other aspects of the discipline include the philosophical foundation of ethics as well as the philosophical foundation of individual areas, such as philosophy of art and philosophy of history.

A Christian philosophy is a contradiction in terms. We Christians must not give ourselves over to the quest for wisdom and truth because we love worldly wisdom. God has revealed himself to us in his Son and his Word. A search for truth beyond God's Word is sin. Ransacking old and new philosophies to collect useful splinters of truth and knowledge is a dubious enterprise; it amounts to abandoning the living fountain and building for oneself cisterns which can hold no water (Jer. 2:13).

This history of philosophy is the history of that human wisdom by which man has suppressed the truth of God in unrighteousness (Rom. 1:18). It is to be assessed spiritually in the light of God's Word. Such an analysis of the history of philosophy is certainly an essential area of study in a Christian university. It is not, however, to be established as a discrete discipline, but should, rather, be part of the larger area of *criticism* (see below). If this is not the case, there is danger of a disastrous shift of emphasis. Philosophy again becomes an end in itself, and "Christian" philosophers are born. Due to understandable commitment to the subject they represent, the teachers then take pains to legitimate a "Christian" philosophy. Their example and zeal draw others away from the simplicity of God's Word into the lofty structures of human thought. Subsuming the history of philosophy within the area of criticism protects teachers and students.

It is true, to be sure, that church fathers such as Augustine used philosophical thought. We should not, however, regard theirs as an encouraging example to emulate, but, rather, a warning to be vigilant that we do not abandon the source of living water. I regard as unfortunate Augustine's statement in *De doctrina christiana* that Christians can use the phantom of pagan sciences like the Israelites used the Egyptians' goods. It needs to be noted in passing that these same Egyptian riches were probably the material out of which the golden calf was made at Sinai. Unfortunately, in Christianity golden calves were made out of the riches of pagan philosophy.

Make Criticism Foundational

"The spiritual man makes judgments about all things, but he himself is not subject to any man's judgment" (1 Cor. 2:15). "Do you not know that the saints will judge the world? And if you are to judge the world, are you not competent to judge trivial cases? Do you not know that we will judge angels? How much more the things of this life!" (1 Cor. 6:2–3).

In the face of attack from the world, we Christians have adopted a defensive posture in the area of Christian belief; we have pursued apologetics. It would be more appropriate to the situation, however, to take up a position of criticism based on God's Word with respect to the world we confront. Since the rise of humanism we have become accustomed to having our faith criticized from every quarter of academic learning. We should at long last consider what God's Word has to say to these same academic areas. After all, in some situations the best defense is a good offense. Moreover, in this way we will avoid seeing ourselves as being on exactly the same footing as the world. We will not be guilty of withholding from the world the clear Word we have been commissioned to proclaim to it.

By God's grace we see in increasing measure today signs of just such clear proclamation on the basis of God's Word. Such authors as Francis Schaeffer and Arthur Ernest Wilder may be given as popular examples, and publications in such series as

Wort und Wissen, Wissen und Leben, and *Tagesfragen* pursue a similar line.[3]

In contrast, *apologetics* takes up and takes issue with direct attacks on God's Word. It has chiefly a defensive function. We can view it as a discipline under the larger heading of criticism, although it is preferable to discuss it in connection with each individual area of study which has come under attack.

I would propose to organize the intellectual domain of criticism in the way outlined in fig. 4.1:[4]

Fig. 4.1 The Intellectual Domain of Criticism

1. criticism of philosophy
2. criticism of contemporary intellectual trends
3. criticism of art
4. criticism of the sciences
   a) general criticism and criticism of philosophies of science
   b) principles, individual theses, or results of special relevance
   c) criticism of the individual scientific disciplines
      (integrated into individual areas of study)
5. apologetics
6. criticism of sins that are particularly in evidence in contemporary
   life (e.g. promiscuity, abortion, homosexuality, the occult
7. criticism of heresies

Design Courses to Enhance Student Ministries

Since the college understands itself as a service organization, the courses of study are to be in line with the students' future goal of ministry. Formal study does not stand in the service of

3. [Recent works published in Germany which approach issues in Christian thought from the general standpoint Linnemann finds helpful and constructive.]

4. [What Linnemann seems to have in mind here and in fig. 4.1 is not merely a negative "critical" exercise but rather a positive enterprise of assessment, discernment, and alternative academic work. In this context criticism may well be understood as critical assessment and reconstruction.]

the self-realization and harmonious development of the personality; its aim is to facilitate the optimal preparation for the ministry that lies ahead.

It is expected that students will focus their own efforts accordingly and exhibit an attitude toward their work that expresses itself in disciplined and efficient study.

Mesh Theory and Praxis, Study and Ministry

Planning the course of study with a view to future ministry leads inevitably to a constant meshing of theory and praxis. This is not only because of what service the student is preparing to accomplish in the future, but also because the student is already called into the Lord's service. Missionary activities and regular occasions for Christian ministry must be firmly embedded in the course of study.

Assess More Than Academic Performance

We need to introduce elsewhere what we have done for some time at the Bible institute in Batu, Indonesia, where I currently teach: The students are assessed not only on the basis of their academic performance but also in view of their spiritual maturity and the quality of their spiritual service.

Organizing a Christian Institution

It is not to be expected that a fully completed educational institution loyal to the Bible can be established in one step. The plan should be to accomplish the goal in stages. Toward this end various foundational issues have already been discussed and settled, and various approaches have been cited.

There are already isolated theological education centers.[5] There also already exist institutions where students can pursue one year of concentrated study from a Christian point of view prior to entering the secular university.[6] Plans are underway in

5. These include: Freie Evangelische-Theologische Akademie, Basel, Switzerland; Freie Theologische Akademie, Gießen, West Germany; Internationales Theologisches Institut, Urk, Netherlands; Evangelische Theologische Faculteit, Heverlee-Leuven, Belgium.

6. For example, Geistliches Rüstzentrum Krelingen (basic theological and language study); Theologisches Vorstudium Breklum. Also: Studiengemeinschaft Wort und Wissen (introductory semester prior to further college study), Gut Holmeke; Evangelische Hogeschule Amersfort, Netherlands (one-year course as basis for further study).

the Netherlands for an eventual full-fledged university. It will be concerned first with the disciplines that have been especially beleaguered by the modern anti-Christian world view and will develop programs first in theology, journalism, and teacher education. Also from the Netherlands comes a useful observation regarding the cost-intensity of various disciplines. Those that can be carried on more inexpensively are to be given preference in initial development.[7]

In light of these various observations, perhaps the following strategy for a sequence of action might be workable:

First stage of development: one year of basic study for students of all disciplines. Part of the content of study would be general, part specifically related to individual disciplines.

Second stage of development: theological education. In addition to basic study, theological training would occur to prepare students as pastors, evangelists, missionaries, and schoolteachers of religion at the primary and secondary levels.[8] There would also be teacher training at the primary level, along with social educational theory, journalism, and possibly basic instruction in church music.

Third stage of development: teacher training. At the secondary level such training would encompass entire disciplines, linguistics, religious studies (including world religions and phenomenology of religion), law, and economics.

Fourth stage of development: further extension. Programs would include the natural sciences, medicine, and pharmaceutics.

7. This viewpoint is argued in van Velzen, "Christelijk Hoger Onderwijs Nieuwe Stijl."

8. [In Germany religion is taught in public schools. "Primary" and "secondary" correspond roughly to American "grade school" and "high school" divisions.]

Excursus 1

General Studies
for Christian Students

Since the modern university rises out of an anti-Christian spirit, we have an urgent need for a university-level Christian education center.

Key features of the education we wish to see offered do not just include teachers and students being serious Christians, placing themselves under God's Word, and praying at the beginning and ending of learning activities. It is also requisite that everything taught and researched be thought through on the basis of the reality of Jesus Christ, in whom all treasures of wisdom and knowledge are hidden (Col. 2:3). Every individual discipline must take its bearings from God's Word. We need an education center which is bound by the truth and grounded in the truth.

Such a reorientation of disciplines is a task whose execution still lies ahead; it will take time. But teachers need the inner motivation to move in this direction, and those heading into higher education stand in urgent need of orientation before they are exposed to the anti-Christian setting of their university studies. Both needs can be adequately met by a one-year course in the form of a Christian college.

The introductory semester offered by Wort und Wissen[1] should not be competitively supplanted by the general studies we envision but included and placed on a broader basis.

The "general studies" designation will facilitate state accreditation by underscoring that we are offering entry level instruction that is not merely discipline-related. Comparable institu-

---

1. [An independent Christian study center in Germany.]

tions in the area of theological instruction are the one-year programs in Breklum and Krelingen.

Organizational Affiliations

There are several reasons for attempting to utilize the resources of a school sponsored by a non-State evangelical association.[2] First, behind such schools stand congregations who could bear the load. They are in the position to carry on the additional work by their prayers and labor. Second, both the schools themselves and other local Christians associated with the schools comprise a strong pool of qualified and competent professionals with expertise that could be utilized in introductory-level higher education. It is important that teachers be local to give the education a continuity which is endangered when teaching is mainly provided by guest lecturers from elsewhere. Third, the facilities and technical resources of such schools are sometimes far superior to those found even in accredited teachers' colleges. In any case they will likely suffice fully for the student activities of the first two semesters. Fourth, the rooms of the schools are, as a rule, not used in the afternoon, and some of them are not filled in the morning.

Community Life

Since the college is defined by the basic principle of discipleship, and since the students should gain practice in this by a binding community life, the college needs more than a school as education center: It also needs a complex of its own to serve as a living center. In the long run it seems reasonable to plan for facilities that would serve two hundred to three hundred students, though at first fifty to seventy would be plenty to get started. The students should obligate themselves to live at the center so that the impression will be comprehensive.

Within smaller student groups in the center, every student should be in quarters with students of various disciplines so that an optimal interdisciplinary exchange can take place. This will

2. [In Germany, as in the USA, many are not completely satisfied with public education. Some Christian groups have therefore banded together to support "non-State" private schools for their children. These groups are what Linnemann means by "non-State evangelical associations."]

also further interdisciplinary connections. These small groups nurture the spiritual life of the larger living center.

The Course of Study

It may prove effective to combine a mixture of scheduled courses and slots to be filled by guest lecturers. In this way continuity may be preserved, and the resources of evangelical scientists from all disciplines may also be fully utilized. Lectures by guest instructors should be mandatory for all students regardless of their particular area of study. Needed introductory material or orientation aids should be made available in consultation with the lecturer. Special lectures should be open to the widest possible audience outside the school. Seminars, in contrast, would be reserved for students of particular subjects, those students whose chosen discipline places them within a discrete group.

The goal is to represent the entire breadth of coverage found in the university. The essential areas of study should be covered. Medicine is within the natural science areas which are encountered at the onset of study. The curriculum could dispense with exotic subjects.

Some lectures can be attended generally by all students. Other lectures are designed for more specific groups of perhaps fifteen to twenty-five students whose disciplines are related. Still others are for groups of five to ten students who share the same discipline. These small groups also conduct Bible studies related to their discipline.

Every student should, therefore, be integrated in a dual sense, interdisciplinarily integrated within the living center and integrated by discipline within the study group.

The plan of study must retain flexibility. Course offerings must be rearranged at times to allow for guest lectures, but this must not interfere with the overall level of instruction.

Educational Objectives

Students should be rooted and grounded in God's Word during this year of study and should make progress in discipleship. All students, regardless of discipline, should receive a good Biblical foundation. They should acquire extensive knowledge about the Bible itself, as well as a systematic grasp of what the Bible teaches.

The students should also gain facility in assessing the training they have received in non-Christian schools from the standpoint of the Christian faith. False premises and the spiritual damage this has caused should be rectified. The fundamental starting points of the anti-Christian spirit in culture and science should be comprehended. The attitude of the student should be steered by a meaningful course of study. This should take place in such a way that he is not alienated from God's Word but rather penetrates it and discovers God's wisdom for all areas of life.

General and specialized academic orientation should result in students acquiring the basic tools for effective further study. The study conditions should lead to a suitable attitude toward academic work and competence in specific disciplines. There needs to be hard work! But the work should be accompanied by more joy and much more effectiveness through meaningful guidance than would be possible in a purely secular setting.

The anti-Christian structure of the university should be critiqued, and students should recognize the extent to which basic premises of so-called science in the various disciplines are in fact simply deductions based on anti-Christian presuppositions. The Christian bases of the various disciplines, properly understood, should be grasped, taking into account viewpoints which may furnish new starting points for a Christian understanding in various disciplines. From such viewpoints new conceptions of disciplines may proliferate on the basis of God's Word.

The university should be viewed as a mission field in its own right.

The General Plan of Study

The curriculum and university experience should be designed around ten elements:

1. Dynamic fellowship under God's Word
2. In-depth information about the Bible
3. Systematic exposure to what the Bible teaches
4. Analysis of the university in its anti-Christian conception (debunking the lie of "value-free science" and uncovering the ideological implications of philosophies of science, as well as the anti-Christian bases and structures of the various disciplines, generally and in specific instances)

5. The Christian bases of the various disciplines, properly understood

6. General orientation in study methods, including, but not limited to: *use of libraries*: ordering of books, how to use various indexes, what bibliographical aids are available for the various disciplines, and how to find and use material on reserve which is to be read in conjunction with lectures; *standard forms* for writing a scientific paper; *pointers on joint research* and attaining suitable thoroughness; *how to use books effectively* —those one owns which can therefore be underlined or consulted easily and those one does not own; *constructing card files*; *rapid reading*, and *effective use of lectures*.

7. Orientation for study in specific disciplines (Allowing further understanding of points 5 and 6). It would include: *modes of inquiry* specific to the discipline; *insight into the construction* of the discipline and its subcategories; *an overview of the foundational literature* of a discipline; *a sensible plan of study, and survival strategy* for coping with the anti-Christian environment of the discipline.

8. Acquisition of information and skills related to specific disciplines through basic courses required before advanced study.

9. Broad but specific introduction to opportunities for missionary service and ongoing activities on the mission field of the university, combined with practical evangelistic activities.

10. Sports and meaningful leisure time pursuits for balance.

Excursus 2

The Dependability of Thought

We are accustomed to regarding thought that is disciplined and regulated by scientific principles as reliable. Further, we are accustomed, not only to distinguishing between faith and thought, but also to separating them from each other, so that faith is banned from the realm of thought, and thought deems itself to be excluded from the realm of faith. Both of these customary viewpoints which we have thoroughly accepted are highly deceptive.

Disciplined, scientifically regulated thought[1] is indeed communicable and thereby makes interpersonal activity possible. It is, however, limited by sin and has cut itself off from the truth by its commitment to anthropocentric and reductionistic (whether dualistic or monistic) modes of thought. Through an anti-Christian decision, thought is so defined as to exclude God. In the perception of reality, the Creator of reality is not permitted to be taken into account. Thought of this description, therefore, despite its ordered logic, has wandered outside the pale of truth.[2]

It is not thought which has cut itself off from the faith that is to be depended on, but rather only that thought which is guided by the faith and grounded in God's Word. Only a person who has experienced the new birth and lives in that fear of God which is the beginning of wisdom can arrive at true knowledge—which is not to deny that science arrives at correct knowledge in certain individual cases.

The student gains the *impression*, nevertheless, that his think-

1. On this point see chapter 7.
2. Lutz von Padberg, "Gegen die Aufspaltung," 4–6.

ing, which has been trained through studies and increasingly regulated by the traditionally accepted premises of the scientific disciplines he has been steeped in, is dependable. In fact the student is only experiencing the proper functioning of the code system that has been appropriated. This system is meant to facilitate communication, at least among those "initiated" into its language.

For those who are not initiated, the use of the code is damaging to communication. The student does not recognize the code for what it is; instead, it is erroneously identified as truth. But the student believes this grand new truth can restore communication to those who are not "initiated." They can be shown how they too can be "in the know." The student becomes a missionary of historical-critical theology or evolutionary natural science.

It is quite understandably assumed by others that the initiated student who has done formal study knows better than lay persons who have not. The "missionary activity," therefore, is highly effective and paves the way for uncertainty and doubt in those influenced.

In short, the student who undergoes or has completed critical study is usually profoundly convinced of the dependability of scientific thought. Today, to be sure, philosophers of science are increasingly aware of the foundational crisis in science,[3] but this crisis is not yet widely known or accepted. The impression still prevails that scientific thought is dependable. This impression, however, does not correspond to reality. At its root lies the confusion between the functional code system, by means of which we have agreed to talk about reality, and reality itself. Reality, however, is the triune God, his creation, and his revelation.

Yet the dependability of thought appears demonstrable, someone will say, in view of its vindication in medicine and technology. We have already spoken of the "two faces" of medical and technological progress. It should nevertheless be pointed out once more that all valid inventions are imitations or applications of the creation God himself has made. The principles God applied in his creation are recognized and applied. At best, then, the natural sciences are a rethinking of God's thoughts. The production of paper out of wood was learned from the wasp, aeronautical principles from birds, the principle of helicopter flight

3. Ibid., 1, 7–10.

from the dragonfly, to name just a few of the most striking examples.

Researchers get their ideas from the creation, and what they invent functions correctly only to the extent that they have correctly applied principles already present in the creation. Insofar as natural scientists deal with "the objective," they are dealing with creation. Through this they have a corrective for their thinking, whether they realize it or not. Their thought is based on something other than their thought.

There exists, however, the danger of perverting the insights gained from God's creation through influences from tendencies which are inimical to God, man, and creation. A hubris arises by which principles discovered in creation are used to exceed the former limits of creation. Jet airplanes, designed on the basis of discoveries made possible by creation, go beyond anything formerly found in creation, with damaging results to the environment.

Similarly, there is the tendency to regard everything that can be explored as something that should be explored. This tendency is not only widely accepted; it is structured into the very essence of the scientific enterprise. Science itself recognizes no boundaries for its investigations. These can only be set for it from the outside. But there has been little success in setting such limits, and in the long run there seems little prospect that any will be set. As long as our society continues to give science the recognition it currently enjoys, it will push for the right to investigate what it wishes, and it will be successful, because that is the judgment God has set for such designs of fallen humanity (see Gen. 11:6: ". . . nothing they plan to do will be impossible for them.") Only on the basis of redemption in Jesus Christ is there the prospect for a measured scholarship which has escaped compulsive preoccupation with "progress." This is vital since, as things stand, results from research are being indiscriminately applied—as atom bombs, biological and chemical weapons, and genetic tampering.

The "useful invention" (for example, the heart-lung machine) cannot be separated from this larger context. In effect the useful invention functions as an alibi for much else that goes on.

The Christian natural scientist, too, is implicated in this structure. He can take pains to obey God within the established parameters of science, but he has no influence on those parameters, not even if his research results gain recognition. They are marked down as "scientific achievements" and credited to the account of science. The natural scientist who is a Christian, it seems to me, can do about as much to influence the general direction of research in the natural sciences as a swimmer can to steer the course of an ocean-going luxury liner by jumping into the ship's pool and swimming in the opposite direction from that of the ship.

If God wills that a regenerate natural scientist labor at his place in the university or research institute, God will certainly make him a blessing there and bless his work. His research will be predominantly positive, while that of someone else in the same role might have had destructive effects. He must, nevertheless, reckon with the possibility that he is also functioning as an alibi and an advertising sign.

What is disastrous is that examples from the natural sciences are used to try to further studies in the humanities. Examples drawn from useful scientific inventions are used as bait to attract students to the fishhooks of philosophy or historical-critical theology. The humanities attempt in this way to capitalize on the natural sciences like a poor man might try to use the name of a millionaire relative to get money for himself.

Natural *science* and *science* in the humanities are, however, not to be equated, though both are associated with the concept of *science*. It is intellectually dishonest for thought in the humanities to operate on the foundation of examples from the natural sciences. That is true even in the practice of taking over definitions. The concept *hypothesis*, for example, in the natural sciences serves an entirely different function than in the humanities, where hypotheses cannot be verified or falsified through experiments. The humanities lack the guiding safeguard of an external created order, if not always totally then at least substantially. The self or "psyche," which psychology attempts to analyze, is an example since it is manipulable. It is not like a chemical composition or biological process. If not grounded in God's Word, the humanities utterly lack objective footing, while the natural sciences possess a corrective at least in the creation.

The exemplary results of findings from the natural sciences which are cited by the humanities are often helpful and appropriately limited in their scope. In contrast, helpful and limited pursuits in the humanities are gladly pushed into the background. The compiling of concordances, lexicons, tabulated oversights of the course of historical events, and much more, are regarded as "donkey-work" of little scientific value. They are gladly used but they are not recognized as "scientific achievement" because they are considered to lack originality.

If one wishes to see clearly what is at issue here one must ask what it is that establishes the name of a scientist. Bultmann, for example, did not gain renown because he made valid statements regarding the use of a few concepts employed by Paul. What made his reputation was his theology and the demythologizing that was part and parcel of it.

In any case, one can only establish a reputation in science within the context of the "tradition," the accepted premises and findings of the past and present. In the natural sciences there is, admittedly, willingness to celebrate the appearance of an innovative, inventive outsider. In the humanities, however, one's only chance is to operate within the traditionally accepted premises—unless someone manages to ride the crest of a popular trend—such as the theology of revolution, which was sustained by Marxist thought. Such tendencies are always fleshly, earthly and diabolical (as observed in James 3:15) unless they are nourished by God's Word during times of spiritual renewal.

The question may be posed: In the so-called hard sciences (mathematics, physics, chemistry, and to a lesser extent biology, geology, pharmaceutics, and medicine), is it not irrelevant to the results of research whether the researcher was a regenerate Christian or a militant atheist? Was it not settled centuries ago in controversies over elementary education that there is no such thing as Catholic mathematics, or Protestant physics?

It is true that *subjective motivations* may count for little in a given research project. The invention of the heart-lung machine arose from the intention to make survival possible in a precisely delineated crisis situation; as a scientific result this invention stands independent of possible subjective motives. It does not matter, finally, whether what spurred the work that led to the invention was the desire for recognition, or ambition, or envy, or whether the sole intention was to help humanity and serve God. In such a case, where a given research project combines with humane good intention, subjective motivations play a subordinate role. In addition, one may surmise that God's blessing may also have been at work.

All specific research, however, occurs within a conceptual framework, which determines the overall direction of research. This conceptual framework decides, for example, what gets investigated and what gets neglected by researchers. One might cite the intensive research into contraceptives and the relative dearth of research into the suffering of the fetus when it is killed in the womb in order to gain the real facts about what happens when a pregnancy is "terminated" in this way.

The direction of research in its entirety, the distribution of projects and means, the enrichment of the spectrum of available methods—these are all steered by the conditions prevailing in a given context. And those conditions vary greatly, depending largely on whether they are determined by an allegedly neutral but in fact atheistically conceived science, or whether they are formed from the standpoint of faith in God, the Creator and Father of our Lord Jesus Christ.

We must distinguish between the conscious, subjective motives and the determinative decisions[4] which (whether the researcher realizes it or not) determine the entire scientific enterprise to the extent that they have received institutional endorsement. The former have less influence; the latter have lasting effect in the long run—unless this effect is slowed or hindered by such external circumstances as the institutional context.

Let us now summarize: Is thinking to be trusted? Thought is not autonomous but *dependent*—not so much in its execution as in its point of departure. It is never absolute; it is never carried on purely of and for itself but is always determined by connections. Thought is dependent on a point outside itself. The theory of the autonomy of thought disregards the fact that man is a creature, created for God and therefore dependent on him. He

4. The edifice of the scientific disciplines consists of solidly cemented (institutionalized), atheistic decisions. Taken as a whole, these may be compared to a framework, made of iron-reinforced concrete, for a wall under construction. Anyone who wishes to lay a stone within this framework may do so—but only within the framework. The basic shape and direction of the wall has already been determined. "Freedom of inquiry" exists only within this structure, which determines what is recognized as legitimate research and what is not. Whoever wants to be a scientist and to have access to research facilities, computers, and laboratories must operate within this structure; whoever requires a scientific publisher for the production of his books must do likewise—unless content to harvest a crop of rejection slips.

can turn away from God, but only by becoming a slave of sin and the flesh, by becoming like the world through and through.

If thinking is only possible in terms of "givens," then the question arises of which "given" I am going to decide to favor. I either decide for God's Word as revealed truth, or I decide for that philosophy which declares itself to be atheistic, which maintains that truth can only be found inductively and established only in the sciences.

I can by no means place great confidence in such earthly-minded thinking as the humanities. When thought in these areas is not grounded in God's Word it degenerates into frivolity. Such thought stands in unconditional need of God's Word as a corrective. It is trustworthy only when grounded on God's Word. The natural sciences have a corrective in the creation and, with reference to it, are in the position to assert limited truths. Only in conjunction with God's Word, however, can human thought be dependable; and that is no less true for the natural sciences than it is for the humanities.

In this connection I would like once more to call attention to Lutz von Padberg's *Prolegomena to a Biblical Epistemology*, mentioned in chapter 4, note one above.[5] There also the question is answered as to whether thought stands in need of redemption.

I would like to supplement in a small way one of his minor points: "Spirit-led knowledge takes place progressively." Von Padberg is primarily addressing the *capacity* to know. Alongside of this one should, it seems to me, consider motives, habits, and structures of thought. The capacity to think is altered (by being restored) through spiritual rebirth. The altering of the motives of thought, the habits of thought, and the structures of thought is, however, a part of sanctification, albeit an often neglected part.

Regarding the altering of *motives,* God's Word tell us: "Therefore, rid yourselves of all malice and all deceit, hypocrisy, envy, and slander of every kind. Like newborn babies, crave pure spiritual milk, so that by it you may grow up in your salvation, now that you have tasted that the Lord is good" (1 Peter

5. At least a few of the other helpful sources I have found in rethinking things include Werner Gitt, *"Das Fundament"*, in *Wissen und Leben*, Vol. 7 (1985); Meskemper, *Falsche Propheten*; Otto Riecker, *Universitätstheologie und Gemeindefrömmigkeit* (Neuhausen-Stuttgart, 1984); Helge Stadelmann, *Grundlinien eines bibeltreuen Schriftverständnisses* (TVG, 1985); Bodo Volkmann, *Das Maß aller Dinge* (Neuhausen-Stuttgart, 1985).

2:1–3). God's Word likewise states: "But now you must rid yourselves of all such things as these: anger, rage, malice, slander,
and filthy language from your lips. Do not lie to each other,
since you have taken off your old self with its practices and have
put on the new self, which is being renewed in knowledge in
the image of its Creator" (Col. 3:8–10). The admonition, we see,
is to get rid of, to lay aside, previous motives. Concerning the
altering of *habits of thought*, we are exhorted in Romans 12:2:
"Do not conform any longer to the pattern of this world, but be
transformed by the renewing of your mind. Then you will be
able to test and approve what God's will is—his good, pleasing,
and perfect will." The admonition here is that we be transformed by the renewal of the mind.

The altering of *structures of thought* can come about only by
rejecting and departing from sites where harmful structures of
thought reign. These structures are not innate to me; I am,
rather, included in them, and I must therefore expressly free
myself from them. We are admonished, then, to "come out from
them" (2 Cor. 6:17).

5

The Bible and Modern Man

The Bible is a very old book, and today what is old no longer commands respect. Yes, one hears talk of how important classical antiquity is; nostalgia is all the rage, and antiques are hot items. But these old items just sit in display cases to be gawked at, increase the pride of the owner, and enhance someone's prestige. For the most part they are regarded as having no practical use. Today, that which is old is generally considered to be outmoded. What counts is what is modern: the latest technological conveniences, the newest scientific findings, the latest news, the new fashions, and other trappings of modern living. To be out of date has come to be a weighty reproach. Everyone wants to be known as a "modern person."

The Meaning of "Modern"

But how modern is the modern person? When I was straightening up my books after a move I picked up a book with the title, *Modern Homiletics*. The book appeared in the early 1920s. Today, no one would regard a product of the 1920s as modern but rather as old-fashioned; the modern person of 1920 now seems to many like a relic of yesteryear. And the modern person of the French Revolution, who enthroned the goddess Reason and worshipped her in cathedrals, truly is a relic of a bygone era.

Accordingly, it appears that modern man is a very relative entity. Still, we do not want to neglect to inquire whether there may be characteristics which distinguish man of earlier ages from man today.

My theology teachers were in the habit of seeing New Testament man (and, of course, all the more so Old Testament man) as mythical, to distinguish him from "modern man, the man of reason." Upon closer scrutiny, however, this so-called mythical man is anything but essentially different from modern man. Certainly those in biblical times did allow for the possibility of miracles; yet miracles were not the order of the day for him, so his reaction to them was astonishment and even terror. Normally he expected things to function according to laws of nature:

Jairus' servants told their master, "Your daughter is dead. Why bother the teacher any more?" (Mark 5:35).

Jesus was laughed at with scorn by the mourning women when he said to them at the deathbed of the girl, "Why all this commotion and wailing? The child is not dead but asleep" (Mark 5:39). The women laughed because, being professional mourners, they were quite able to know a corpse when they saw one.

Or consider the response when Jesus gave the command to move the stone from the entrance to Lazarus' tomb. "'But Lord,' said Martha, the sister of the dead man, 'by this time there is a bad odor, for he has been there four days'" (John 11:39).

The miracles of resuscitation which Jesus worked occurred in the presence of persons who were thoroughly familiar with the regularities of death. Of course they could not yet monitor death's approach with instruments which show essential body functions. However, if that were the requirement for being a modern person, then only the contemporary medical technologists who manufacture such devices are modern, along with the doctors and nurses who use them: Few of us could qualify.

People in Jesus' time were also able to make meteorological predictions based on their observations. Jesus assumed this when he said, "When you see a cloud rising in the west, immediately you say, 'It's going to rain,' and it does. And when the south wind blows, you say, 'It's going to be hot,' and it is" (Luke 12:54–55.). Obviously, back then they had no weather satellites and sophisticated measuring instruments for weather forecasting. However, if such instrumentation were the requirement for being a modern person, meteorologists would qualify, but reading the barometer on our wall comes a bit short of certifying the rest of us as meteorologists.

The person in Bible times was also aware of what we call economics. For in view of the impending seven years' famine which was to follow seven years of plenty, Joseph gave this counsel:

> And now let Pharaoh look for a discerning and wise man and put him in charge of the land of Egypt. Let Pharaoh appoint commissioners over the land to take a fifth of the harvest of Egypt during the seven years of abundance. They should collect all the food of these good years that are coming and store up the grain under the authority of Pharaoh, to be kept in the cities for food. This food should be held in reserve for the country, to be used during the seven years of famine that will come upon Egypt, so that the country may not be ruined by the famine. [Gen. 41:33–36]

Tractors and combines were unheard of back then; that is true. But I wonder how many of you could build one of these machines or even know how to run them? Is technology really that which defines what it means to be modern?

Even a person from Papua, New Guinea, who still may live in what we consider Stone Age conditions, figures out fairly quickly the connection between a light switch and the light which shines from an electric light bulb. Countless people from our surroundings who are without question "modern" have little more understanding of technology than how to flick a light switch. The urban New Guinean living in Djakarta may draw up construction plans in his office for a state-of-the-art rice planter. Yet in his new house in the modern quarter of the city he makes use of fetishes which bind him to demons. Is that a "modern man"?

That is Indonesia. But how is it in Europe and North America? Every residence is equipped with the most modern electric and electronic gadgets. In offices and factories the most modern machines are in use. After just a few years such machinery is obsolete and needing replacement. If one can possibly manage, one drives the very latest model car. Even when one opts instead to purchase an antique, say a Model T Ford, one is still just following a current fashion—antique cars are "in"!

By that standard we really are modern. Modern literature and modern art are disseminated even at the elementary school level. People want their marriages to be modern and to think modern in every area of life. At the same time, however, the most ancient superstitions are still alive and well. Many "knock on wood"; when they do so in Germany they say "toi, toi, toi," which means "devil, devil, devil." People cross their fingers (or in Germany hold their thumbs) and are leery of Friday the thirteenth and certain other days on the calendar. In the West at New Year's, just like in ancient China, huge fireworks displays disperse the evil spirits. Many people still think their day is ruined by a black cat passing in front of them in the wrong direction.

Yet it is not merely old superstition that is in vogue. New superstition has gained the upper hand and flourishes as a result of today's widespread renunciation of faith in our Lord and Savior Jesus Christ.

- So-called "modern man" busies himself with horoscopes (even, it is reported, in the White House!) and visits seers. Cheap junkmail advertising delivered to our homes offers the services of astrologers and fortunetellers.
- In Germany, popular illustrated magazines with large circulations have for years carried ads for amulets that promise good fortune and health.
- Occult practices, "Ouija" boards, and the like have become popular as party games.
- The occult cross of Nero, the satanic counterpart to the cross on which our Lord Jesus Christ bore the sin of the entire world, is used as a sign of the struggle against nuclear armaments and is scribbled on walls as a peace symbol.
- In transcendental meditation people receive their mantra and meditate, whether they know it or not, on verses which were composed to honor Hindu deities.
- Magical practices find broad and even planned dissemination in our contemporary culture.
- Satanic cults are increasingly and openly popular.

Is the employer who owns an elaborate, fully electronic industrial installation and relaxes with transcendental meditation a "modern man"? Is the dashing race car driver with an amulet around his neck and a St. Christopher charm around his wrist a "modern man"? Is the political radical with his can of paint and spray gun a "modern man" as he defaces walls with occult symbols?

How should we then regard the following commonly heard statements, which have gained currency in theology since the Enlightenment? "A modern person cannot understand the doctrine of the substitutionary atonement for sin through the death of Jesus Christ." "It is impossible to expect a modern person who uses a light switch to believe in angels and demons." (A point of clarification: Christians do not *believe* in angels or demons, but rather on God the Father, the Son, and the Holy Spirit. They know, however, from God's Word that angels and demons exist.) How about this claim: "The standards set forth in the Bible no longer apply to modern people"?

What are we to make of the widespread manner of speaking which starts out: "It is impossible for a modern person to . . ."? It is assumed that someone presently alive and nonetheless engaged in a certain action or activity is not a "modern person," but is rather antiprogressive—although with enough exposure to enlightened thinking and the required peer pressure that person just might come around and finally see the light.

In view of the relativity of the concepts *modern* and *modern person*, it is fair to say that such manners of speaking theologically as cited above, with their mingling of relativistic and absolutistic thinking, are unfounded slogans having demagogic character.

In the Last Days

The modern man allegedly wishes to know nothing about the Bible. Does the Bible know anything about modern man?

The approach to what is modern today, dated tomorrow, and obsolete the next day is seen in the Bible for what it is, "chasing after the wind" (Eccles. 1:14). God's judgment in this matter is clear: "There is nothing new under the sun" (Eccles. 1:9).

God's Word, however, also talks about a modern man who overtakes and replaces the modern man of 1525, 1789, 1848, 1918, 1945, 1984, and so on. That is, it speaks about man in the last days, before God's mighty final judgment engulfs this earth, and after which our Lord Jesus, the Son of man, appears as judge. God's Word says two things about man in the final days:

This man basically does not live any differently than man before him has lived. What comprises life remains constant, as

Jesus states, "As it was in the days of Noah, so it will be at the coming of the Son of Man. For in the days before the flood, people were eating and drinking, marrying and giving in marriage, up to the day Noah entered the ark; and they knew nothing about what would happen until the flood came and took them all away. That is how it will be at the coming of the Son of Man" (Matt. 24:37–39). Or as Jesus explains elsewhere, "It was the same in the days of Lot. People were eating and drinking, buying and selling, planting and building. But the day Lot left Sodom, fire and sulfur rained down from heaven and destroyed them all. It will be just like this on the day the Son of Man is revealed" (Luke 17:28–30).

Man of the last days, man who will never be overtaken by another generation, lives just as the many generations before lived, eating, drinking, marrying, buying, selling, planting, and building. This "normal" human life, which is not wrong in itself, is fateful in view of its blindness to the signs of the times. There is contentment with the purely physical dimensions of life and total apathy toward the spiritual—toward God and what he expects. This approach to life stands under God's judgment:

> The wrath of God is being revealed from heaven against all the godlessness and wickedness of men who suppress the truth by their wickedness, since what may be known about God is plain to them, because God has made it plain to them. For since the creation of the world God's invisible qualities—his eternal power and divine nature—have been clearly seen, being understood from what has been made, so that men are without excuse.
>
> For although they knew God, they neither glorified him as God nor gave thanks to him, but their thinking became futile and their foolish hearts were darkened. . . .
>
> Therefore God gave them over in the sinful desires of their hearts to sexual impurity for the degrading of their bodies with one another. They exchanged the truth of God for a lie, and worshiped and served created things rather than the Creator—who is forever praised. Amen. . . .
>
> Furthermore, since they did not think it worthwhile to retain the knowledge of god, he gave them over to a depraved mind, to do what ought not to be done" (Rom. 1:18–21, 24–25, 28).

God's Word sketches a clear portrait of man in the last days, man who will never be overtaken by those who would have come after. In this portrait those striking features which distinguish this generation from earlier generations are highlighted:

> But mark this: There will be terrible times in the last days. People will be lovers of themselves, lovers of money, boastful, proud, abusive, disobedient to their parents, ungrateful, unholy, without love, unforgiving, slanderous, without self-control, brutal, not lovers of the good, treacherous, rash, conceited, lovers of pleasure rather than lovers of God—having a form of godliness but denying its power. Have nothing to do with them.
>
> They are the kind who worm their way into homes and gain control over weak-willed women, who are loaded down with sins and are swayed by all kinds of evil desires, always learning but never able to acknowledge the truth. Just as Jannes and Jambres opposed Moses, so also these men oppose the truth—men of depraved minds, who, as far as the faith is concerned, are rejected. [2 Tim. 3:1–8]

Isn't it amazing how apt a description this is of man today? It is instructive to place this description alongside the daily paper for comparison!

The spirit of the Antichrist has gained a prominent place in modern man. God's Word says of him: "Who is the liar? It is the man who denies that Jesus is the Christ. Such a man is the antichrist—he denies the Father and the Son" (1 John 2:22). It also states: "Dear friends, do not believe every spirit, but test the spirits to see whether they are from God, because many false prophets have gone out into the world. This is how you can recognize the Spirit of God: Every spirit that acknowledges that Jesus Christ has come in the flesh is from God, but every spirit that does not acknowledge Jesus is not from God. This is the spirit of the antichrist, which you have heard is coming and even now is already in the world" (1 John 4:1–3).

"And we have seen and testify that the Father has sent his Son to be the Savior of the world" (1 John 4:14). That is the confession of faith. Yet it has become rare in the church and in theology. Where it is still repeated on Sundays, to a large extent mere lip-service is involved; every person distinguishes within himself what he really believes from that which he is saying.

God's Word foretold what the theology of modern man, the man of the last days, would look like:

> But there were also false prophets among the people, just as there will be false teachers among you. They will secretly intro-

duce destructive heresies, even denying the sovereign Lord who bought them—bringing swift destruction on themselves. Many will follow their shameful ways and will bring the way of truth into disrepute. In their greed these teachers will exploit you with stories they have made up. Their condemnation has long been hanging over them, and their destruction has not been sleeping. [2 Pet. 2:1–3]

Another passage sounds the same alarm:

For certain men whose condemnation was written about long ago have secretly slipped in among you. They are godless men, who change the grace of our God into a license for immorality and deny Jesus Christ our only Sovereign and Lord. . . .

These men are grumblers and faultfinders; they follow their own evil desires; they boast about themselves and flatter others for their own advantage.

But, dear friends, remember what the apostles of our Lord Jesus Christ foretold. They said to you, "In the last times there will be scoffers who will follow their own ungodly desires." These are the men who divide you, who follow mere natural instincts and do not have the Spirit. [Jude 4, 16–19]

God's Word issues a clear directive: "Understand that in the last days scoffers will come, scoffing and following their own evil desires. They will say, 'Where is this "coming" he promised? Ever since our fathers died, everything goes on as it has since the beginning of creation'" (2 Pet. 3:3–4).

God knows modern man; he saw through him long ago. The allegedly antiquated Bible has long since made plain how things stand with the most modern of all modern generations, the man of the end times. He is manifest before God and can in the Bible read all about what God thinks of him!

Do we find this situation frightening? Perhaps our sentiments are reflected in the meditation of Psalm 139:1–7:

O LORD, you have searched me
and you know me.
You know when I sit and when I rise;
you perceive my thoughts from afar.
You discern my going out and my lying down;
you are familiar with all my ways.
Before a word is on my tongue
you know it completely, O LORD.

You hem me in—behind and before;
you have laid your hand upon me.
Such knowledge is too wonderful for me,
too lofty for me to attain.
Where can I go from your Spirit?
Where can I flee from your presence?

There is a place of refuge where we can hide ourselves from God's wrath, which rightly awaits our sin: It is our Savior Jesus Christ and his work on Golgotha. Let us respond to him right now. "Today, if you hear his voice, do not harden your hearts . . ." (Ps. 95:7–8).

Jesus Christ went to the cross for the sin of our godlessness and for the innumerable sins that resulted from our godless state. He hung there in our place. In our place he endured the wrath of our Creator. "The punishment that brought us peace was upon him" (Isa. 53:5). God himself gave his beloved Son as the sacrificial lamb for us: "For God so loved the world that he gave his one and only Son, that whoever believes in him shall not perish but have eternal life" (John 3:16).

Eternal life—that is not merely "life after death." It is the precious, amazing, meaningful, and fulfilled life which God grants to those who walk the path of the imitation of Jesus. It is life in eternity, which flows into a glorious and joyful existence in God's very presence.

Whoever takes Jesus into his life is given clearance from God to be his child (John 1:12). Can we really comprehend what it means to be children of him who made heaven and earth? The gloriousness of it is still hidden. But one day it will all come to light.

Be reconciled to God, who has everything in place for you. Accept his great gift, his dear Son, sacrificed for our sins and resurrected for our justification (Rom. 4:25). In giving us him God grants us all things (Rom. 8:32).

But you should be aware of this: When Jesus becomes your Savior, then he also is your Master. He intends to rule over your life. That is the only way he can bring something good out of your life—to the praise of his glory. No longer must you be dominated by vice, sin, and carnal appetites. You need no longer be a victim of the fear of death all your life. You shall be guided and led by the Good Shepherd who loves you.

Part 2

God's Word and
Historical-Critical Theology

6

The Study
of Historical-Critical Theology

Some have taken issue with the terminology used in the title for this chapter. They say, "You ought to write, "The Study of the Historical-Critical Method." Much could be said in response to that; I restrict myself to two observations:

One is that the term *historical-critical theology* is eminently justifiable in the framework of general language usage. If, for example, someone in Germany says that he is going to a *Kneippkur*, everyone knows what that means; he is heading for a health resort where he will receive various sorts of hydrotherapies. To be exact, of course, he ought to say that he is going to a health resort in which he will receive treatment according to the methods of the erstwhile Pastor Kneipp. But every German knows that a *Kneippkur* involves these methods and that these methods are what distinguish it from other health resorts.

It is the same in theology. Theology as it is taught in universities all over the world today, both in the East and West as well as in the North and South, is based on the historical-critical method. This holds true especially for the theology taught in Germany, which monopolizes the state universities and claims to be the sole legitimate spokesman on the subject. And the historical-critical method is not just the foundation for the exegetical disciplines. It also decides what the systematician can say and whether one accepts his claims. It determines procedure in Christian education, homiletics, and ethics. It may be that those who are most affected by it are not acutely conscious of it. Yet the historical-critical has truly permeated the theology taught in universities like yeast permeates a lump of sour-dough. If, however, one must work constantly with sourdough, one probably does not notice the smell after a while, even though it is quite noticeable to someone else.

I would also observe that my former colleagues with whom I had contact at meetings of the Society for New Testament Studies would strongly protest if they were ranked as historical-critical methodologists and not as theologians. For they under-stand themselves as theologians and want to be taken seriously as such. Well, in that case there can be no objection to regarding their work as historical-critical theology, instead of speaking merely of historical-critical methodology.

Much more could be said, but let us leave it at that for now and get to the real point.

Theology as Science

The Basic Principle

Research is conducted *ut si Deus non daretur* ("as if there were no God"). That means the reality of God is excluded from con-sideration from the start, even if the researcher acknowledges that God could bear witness of himself in his Word. The stan-dard by which all is assessed is not God's Word but scientific principle. Statements in Scripture regarding place, time, sequences of events, and persons are accepted only insofar as they fit in with established assumptions and theories. Scientific principle has come to have the status of an idol.

The Relativity of the Bible

The presupposition of this scientific theology is the incorpora-tion of the Bible and the Christian faith onto precisely the same level of comparison as other religions and their holy scriptures. Even when that which is distinctive about Christianity is emphasized, the fundamental presupposition remains the gen-eral comparative religions approach. The level of comparison to which Christianity has been reduced, however, is not in itself a fact or some necessary given; it is rather an abstraction, an artifi-cial construct at which one arrives by turning away from the liv-ing God. Anyone who studies scientific theology will inevitably be pushed in the direction of accepting this false assumption.

The concept *Holy Scripture* is relativized so that the Bible is nothing more than a religious writing like all other religious writings. Since other religions have their holy scriptures, one cannot assume that the Bible is somehow unique and superior to them. This is why it gets treated like any other book. There comes to be no distinction between how the Bible is regarded and how the *Odyssey* is read, even though it is clear enough upon careful study that there are differences between them.

To be fair, some think that they serve the proclamation of the gospel when they establish such differences. But they overlook the fact that in the process of making the comparison they reduce God's Word to a collection of religious ideas and theological concepts. This renders the living Word a dead letter, as becomes abundantly clear in many pulpits as pastors strive in vain to bring life to now lifeless texts, resorting finally to psychology, sociology, socialism, and other "-isms" in an attempt to infuse texts with new vitality.

The Bible is no longer esteemed as God's Word in the way it is handled. *It is taken for granted that the words of the Bible and God's words are not identical.* The printed matter between the two covers of the Bible is said not to be God's Word in and of itself. It becomes God's Word only from time to time when it functions as such through reading or preaching. Further, *the New Testament is pitted against the Old Testament*, assuming that the God of the New Testament is different from that of the Old, since Jesus is said to have introduced a new concept of God. Paul is pitted against James. It is also maintained that Acts presents a different Paul from the one who wrote Romans, Galatians, 1 and 2 Corinthians, and other epistles. Acts is often regarded as having merely literary worth; the historical veracity of what Luke reports there is taken just as lightly as the theology he champions. Indeed, every sentence is suspected of containing Luke's theology rather than a reliable report of what actually happened, and that theology is presented as practically the obverse of good theology. Using grotesque literary methods which would lead immediately to absurd results if they were ever applied to the work of a poet or a theologian—say a Goethe, or Barth—claims of inauthenticity are established for the pastoral letters (1 and 2 Timothy and Titus), Ephesians, and Colossians. These claims are then, without careful examination, passed on from one generation of theologians to the next. Differences between individual books of Holy Scripture are blown out of proportion and played up as inconsistencies.

Since the inspiration of Scripture is not accepted, neither can it be assumed that the individual books of Scripture complement each other. Using this procedure one finds in the Bible only a handful of unrelated literary creations. True, it may be acknowledged that in such creations the faith of their authors comes to light. But there is no willingness to recognize in them the One toward whom the author is directing his faith. In other words, they are not considered to be revelation. They are regarded merely as literary and theological creations. As such—two to three thousand years old, written by ancient writers for ancient readers, reflecting conditions alleged by historical-critical investigation to be totally different from those of our own time—they are certified to be anything but contemporary in their relevance.

In order to do justice to the claim of authority which the Biblical canon has for the church, and also for personal orientation, one seeks a "canon within the canon." A few come up with little more than Romans 7, the Good Samaritan in Luke 10, and the parable of final judgment in Matthew 25. For others this "canon within the canon" extends further. In either case, this standard is used to assess the rest of the Bible, and *Sachkritik*[1] is employed, whether explicitly or implicitly. Using Romans, the book of James is devalued. First Corinthians 15:5–8 is criticized using Paul's teachings on faith found elsewhere; it is claimed that Paul is not adhering to the high standards of his own theological insights stated in other passages, because he speaks of the resurrection of Jesus as if it were a historical fact.

Since the content of biblical writings is seen as merely the creations of theological writers, any given verse is nothing more than a non-binding, human theological utterance. John 3:16, for example, becomes only the theological sentiment of an early Christian theologian who penned his gospel near the end of the first century. He was, furthermore, either a gnostic (that is, a heretic), or someone who used gnostic terminology to combat gnosticism, or perhaps someone just more-or-less influenced by gnosticism, which advocated an anti-Christian or quasi-Christian teaching of salvation. In other words, for historical-

---

1. [*Sachkritik* is a method in which what is deemed to be of central importance is used as a standard against which other parts of the Bible are measured. For examples, see p. 149 below.]

critical theology John 3:16 is not a binding, saving promise from God. It is, rather, nothing more than a nonbinding human opinion. All the promises of the Bible are handled in just the same way, although according to God's Word they are all "Yes" and "Amen" in Jesus Christ (2 Cor. 1:20).

The Interpretation of Scripture

The Holy Scripture is regarded as "text" which requires interpretation. It is not disputed, in this view, that we have direct access to Scripture. But what we gain from it is called in question as subjective, "existential" interpretation which is binding only for the interpreter himself. Without going through the passage using historical-critical interpretation, what it yields is declared to be permissible only for private use.

Responsible interpretation for others, as in preaching and teaching, must proceed "methodologically," according to rules, so that it is controllable. The Holy Spirit, who acts as he see fit (see John 3:8), is pushed aside "because no one can guarantee at any time that he has him" as Rudolf Bultmann put it. The Spirit is replaced by the method of interpretation, which is supposed to guarantee the objectivity of the interpretation and its suitability for the biblical text in question.

Nevertheless, he who sits in heaven defies those who champion this approach. Apart from a few basic assumptions and some methodological agreement, one can be certain that where two theologians compare their results, two different conclusions will, as a rule, surface. In contrast, where Bible teachers who take God's Word literally in dependence on the Holy Spirit share what they have gleaned, the unity in spirit and agreement in teaching is continually evident—regardless of confession, continent, and time period.

The undeclared yet working basic principle of Old Testament and New Testament science is: What the text clearly states can, by no means, be true. The exegete's task is to *discover* and *solve* "difficulties" in the text of the Bible. The better the interpreter, the more ingenious this will be. For to amount to anything a professor must "make a name." This is obligatory unless he is content to draw his paycheck without doing what is expected of a professor. The predicament is that it is necessary to strive for human recognition, even if the professor is characteristically disinterested in such accolades. I will gladly vouch that most of my former colleagues are personally rather humble and modest. However, through the system of university theology they are under compulsion to make a name for themselves and to strive for human honor. Yet our Lord Jesus says, "How can you believe if you accept praise from one another, yet make no effort to obtain the praise that comes from the only God?" (John 5:44).

A theology student who has not yet died to the need for the recognition of men stands under the same pressure. Small wonder, then, that many believing theology students soon have grave difficulties in their faith. Often they drift away from the faith without realizing it themselves. Some of what they are learning sticks with them; how could it be otherwise? After all, that is why they are studying! Lines are drawn through parts of God's Word. Some of what it says is no longer believed, and its power is accordingly no longer experienced as it was before. "Paul is not the source of the pastoral epistles," one learns. "The author of the Gospel of John is, of course, not the son of Zebedee, the disciple of Jesus." "The Pentateuch was not written by Moses but compiled from various sources." Anybody who has not learned all this by the sixth semester is regarded with pity, if not scorn, and thus the vineyard is ruined by the little foxes as in Song of Solomon 2:15. It all looks so harmless: These are only trifles; what is at stake is not decisive for the faith. But the authority of God's Word is thereby called in question. It loses its binding character, as becomes swiftly evident with respect to those passages which make us uncomfortable. Let us make no mistake; even a mouse hole can endanger a dike. That becomes clear when a storm brings high water.

Critical Reason and Reality

For historical-critical theology, critical reason decides what is reality in the Bible and what cannot be reality; and this decision is made on the basis of the everyday experience accessible to every person. Nothing is accepted as fact unless it is generally held to be possible. That which is spiritual is judged using fleshly criteria. Experiences of God's children are totally disregarded.

Due to the presuppositions that are adopted, critical reason loses sight of the fact that the Lord, our God, the Almighty, reigns. One is obviously not even in the position to take account of modern-day miracles, even if they are plausibly attested and medically proven. A major reason for this is that the books which glorify the Lord by reporting such incidents will only be handled by certain publishers. These are publishers whose publications are disparaged by historical-critical theologians. As a matter of principle and without personally examining the evidence, the theologians write them off as popular religious drivel.

In its own eyes, historical-critical theology wants to lend assistance to the proclamation of the gospel through an interpretation of the Bible that is scientifically reliable and objective. There is, however, a monstrous contradiction between what it says it wants to do, on the one hand, and what it actually does, on the other. In light of all I have already said, it should be patently obvious that the manner in which historical-critical theology handles the Bible does not further the proclamation of the gospel, but rather hinders it—in fact, it even prevents it. But worse yet, it is by no means clear that we are dealing here with an approach that yields objective and scientifically reliable interpretation of the Scripture as it claims. It is simply not true that historical-critical theology has replaced subjective impressions with a well-grounded discovery of the truth through careful weighing of arguments.

The contradiction between theory and practice, between ideal and reality, shows itself already when one becomes familiar with the pertinent literature. In theory all relevant historical-critical publications on a given theme would be taken into account. In practice this turns out to be impossible due to the constantly growing flood of publications.

How far back one's investigation goes must be given an arbitrary cut-off point. The limit is usually either 1900 or perhaps 1945. In the period 1900–1945, only selected classics of historical-critical theology receive mention. Very, very few works written before 1900 are considered. Although historical-critical theology is practiced today in virtually all countries and continents, the full range of publications remains neglected, because the various writings are composed in languages which not everyone can read. For many English- and German-speaking researchers, French publications already constitute a barrier which many take the trouble to hurdle only if a work is an absolutely indispensable classic. And who undertakes the linguistic preparation required to study books penned by colleagues in modern Greek, Spanish, or Japanese—just to name a few examples? Historical-critical theology's search for truth already stumbles at the point of so much linguistically inaccessible literature which it must neglect.

In addition it is often difficult even to procure literature that is known and accessible. It can take months for something to arrive using interlibrary loan systems. Explicitly or implicitly, the scope of research is restricted to "the literature accessible to me." Many have resorted to a new means of dealing with the flood of literature. Linguists especially favor this method, in which literature that does not employ the same particular methods which a given scholar favors is excluded as a matter of principle.

More and more one observes the use of still another questionable tactic to get around dealing with literature which, given its theme, obviously ought to be worked through intensively: A relevant book is cited, and after a distorted summary a few lines in length it is so negatively assessed that there appears to be no need to pay further attention to it. This way a scholar can spare himself labor which might delay the publication of his own work by years. In view of the prevailing conditions, one can justify this tactic as academic self-defense. Nevertheless, this procedure effectively writes off as "unworthy of discussion" books accepted as dissertations and thereby endorsed by well-known theological faculties—a state of affairs which does not seem to have received adequate attention.

We conclude that we need look no further than how literature is employed to call into serious question the much-vaunted objectivity of historical-critical theology.

The claim that truth is discovered on the basis of critical argumentation is another self-deception. Mutually opposing hypotheses can usually be supported by arguments of somewhat equal weight, sometimes even by the same researcher. Depending on how one regards the established authorities or evidences in a given area, one will be impressed mainly by that which confirms one's own assumptions. If opposing arguments are scrutinized in the investigation, they inevitably turn out to be unconvincing. Such scrutiny, therefore, tends only to corroborate and stabilize one's own thesis.

The basic willingness of historical-critical Bible interpretation to regard its own theses as provisional and debatable by no means implies that the real intent is to establish the truth. In the isolated instance where a viewpoint is altered—which occurs especially seldom with scholars of rank—new arguments, just as persuasive as the old ones but supporting the new position, are adduced. Reason in academics, one could conclude, is susceptible to prostitution.[2]

In scholars' dealings with each other, apart from publications, the overwhelming tendency is to maintain positions already adopted. When one sends a publication to an established scholar for review, a normal response is, "Your remarks are very interesting, but I cannot go along with them." No reasons for this are given. That is not a character flaw but a reaction growing naturally out of the way things are. The professor in his teaching must cover a relatively wide area. He must be in a position to assimilate findings from the entire range of both Old and New Testament research. He can, however, at any given time only pursue in depth such questions as pertain to the small specialized area on which he happens to be working. Even there his deliberations are largely determined by his previous investigations, so that any acceptance of new ideas would demand an excessive amount of revision of formerly held views. Such revision is not to be expected when so many other professorial duties beckon, such as lecturing, administrative work, evaluations of exams and essays, supervision of dissertations, completion of one's own publications, and the editing of contributions to journals.

For these reasons, the acceptance of results from more recent research by scholars who have already formed an opinion in a broad area is inevitably arbitrary. The name of the author of a publication and the school to which he belongs often determine how a publication is received. Under these presuppositions, the vaunted objectivity of historical-critical interpretation of the Bible is doomed to failure from the outset.

2. [What is wrong with adducing new arguments to support a new position? Possibly nothing. But Linnemann's point is how arbitrary the defense of theological positions can be. An "objective" and "scientific" theologian argues confidently, even vehemently, for one position this week, and just as confidently and vehemently for an opposing view the next. When the subject is the eternal truth of God's Word, and when the theologian's rationality "serves as a whore" (*ist nun einmal eine Hure* in Linnemann's words) to legitimize each new position taken, then some skepticism toward "new" arguments and positions may be justified.]

Truth and Subjectivity

Among the upcoming generation of scholars a resignation regarding the truth often prevails. This resignation shows itself in theories of subjectivity. Actually, the logical corollary of this ought to be the end of scientific work in theology, but this conclusion is not taken seriously. The question arises, though, whether science is serving merely as a means of self-realization. One should not overlook, however, the good conscience that theological faculties can maintain about their work in view of the relation between supply and demand which exists as long as churches generally make formal study in these faculties a binding requirement.

Increasingly the younger generation of theologians is being infiltrated by socialism. God's saving purpose and eternal redemption in Jesus Christ are replaced by human goals of world improvement. These goals are veiled in arbitrarily selected words of the so-called "historical Jesus," who is interpreted as social reformer or as revolutionary, depending on what the interpreter desires. Preferred texts include the parable of the Good Samaritan (Luke 10:25–37) and the discourse on world judgment (Matt. 25: 31–46), as well as Jesus' words regarding the Sabbath (Mark 2:27–28). In the last passage the term *son of man* in verse 28 is taken to mean simply *man*, which is linguistically possible. Jesus' table fellowship with tax collectors and sinners (e.g. Mark 2:15–17) is taken as proof that he changed unjust social structures and that we should imitate him in this.

Characteristic of this approach is the theory of *projection*. The Old Testament is for the most part set aside as irrelevant to us because it is, entirely or in part, merely an intellectual construction, a projection. It is the result of then-current patriarchal social structures and reflects ancient agrarian production conditions; the Old Testament had the function of justifying and lending stability to these structures and conditions. According to this theory, even the ten commandments are no longer normative for us. Jesus is said to have abolished them with the commandment to love. But what love means is not derived from God's Word, but is rather determined by sensual means.

The prophets are ranked as social reformers. Amos serves as the alibi for this.

The Practice of Historical-Critical Theology

Like every science, theology is dependent on hypotheses. A hypothesis is an assumption that something is or behaves a certain way. In the natural sciences empirical observations serve to ground assumptions about regularities in the natural realm. These observations are verified by experiments. In the humanities, by contrast, hypotheses have by no means the same function and cannot be verified in the same manner. Both Old and New Testament studies, as science, have taken up as their own, in addition to other methods, the general approaches used in critical historiography and literary criticism.

Critical Historiography

In critical historiography ancient remains and linguistic evidences are used as sources for information about a bygone era, to which one dates the remains and evidences. In such dating assumptions are already at work. This is an important component in the formation of hypotheses. Two examples will illustrate this:

First, if one assumes that the parable of the ten virgins (Matt. 25:1–13) was not spoken by Jesus himself, but rather that it first arose in the early church, then one places it in a different context. It gives information, not about Jesus, but about the early church. To analyze it one compares it to what is known of the early church, not to what is known about Jesus.

Second, if one assumes, on the basis of the differences between John's Gospel and the three other Gospels, that the author of John is not John the disciple of Jesus, then a series of inferences naturally follows: In this case the author himself did not personally experience what he asserts about Jesus. He must have modeled his presentation on earlier sources. This raises the questions about the nature of these earlier documents. And this in turn raises the further question of how John's Gospel is distinct from the sources it is based upon.

Now further assumptions must come into play in relation to the Gospel's theology and bias, as well as the nature of the community which it reflects. Along with this, questions crop up regarding the historical background from a comparative religions point of view; here the task is to distinguish between John's own outlook and that of his sources. What are the major influences on the author of John's Gospel? Gnosticism? Qumran? Judaism with gnostic tendencies? Or is the author taking his bearings mainly from the Old Testament? If his sources are gnostic, how does he relate to them: Polemically? Positively? Critically?

Literary Criticism

In literary criticism the formation of hypotheses has a different function. Answers are sought to questions about the structure and tradition history of the text. Such questions as these, among others, play an important role: Is the text shaped by oral factors, or was it fixed in written form from the beginning? Was it then passed along orally or in writing? Is it a literary unity or not? Does it reflect written sources, or a unified complex of traditions composed of various individual traditions, or particular individual traditions alone? Does it show signs of literary dependence? Has it been editorially reworked, perhaps a number of times? Are there recognizable patterns in the way that individual literary units have been connected?

These are random questions and not a comprehensive list. Every such question is answered on the basis of assumptions. Not one of the assumptions admits to definitive verification. They are merely shown to be tenable through their plausibility and through the researcher's artistry of grounding his assumptions in argumentation. They become acceptable to other researchers by fitting in well within the various complexes of assumptions that are already more or less accepted. Their acceptability derives from their carefully established connections with previous research. In other words: The formation of hypotheses in Old and New Testament science is a self-stabilizing system.

This amounts to an idle toying with God's Word which is not seeking God, even if the individual researcher is convinced that he is rendering a service to God. Work and privation are very much involved—a sixty-hour work-week is common for such a researcher—and this level of effort goes on all one's life, until intellectual and physical strength fail. In order for this lifework not to be in vain, the Old or New Testament scholar's hypotheses must receive recognition. He must strive to receive honor. The only thing that gives this work—which requires so much effort and sacrifice—the appearance of reality is this process of giving and receiving honor from others.

The Results of Research

On the basis of his work the theology professor inevitably gains the secure conviction that God's Word cannot be understood without careful use of the hypothetical constructs of Old and New Testament science. Of this he is truly convinced and is therefore able to pass this conviction on to listeners.

Since students cannot possibly attain the same range of command of the "results of research" which the professor has mastered through years of study, they become insecure and lapse into dependence on whatever the professor says. Rather than asking, not just ritualistically but truly expectantly, the Holy Spirit to open up God's Word to them, they grab a commentary, a work which "explains" a book of the Bible verse by verse in the light of historical criticism. Their study has so conditioned them to find difficulties in the text that they no longer can conceive of working out the meaning of a text without the assistance of commentary.

All it takes to trigger the need to look up what the experts say is for the student who reads a Biblical passage to recall just one critical hypothesis. For critical assumptions are closely knit together, and bringing in one of them tends to call forth them all.

The theology student is generally incapable of detecting what God is saying in his Word, and so passes on to his congregation the conviction with which he has been indoctrinated: Holy Scripture yields its meaning only through use of the historical-critical method. Parishioners receive a condensed version of what was learned in college.

The more effort taken to attain this knowledge, the more precious it becomes. In addition, his knowledge brings the honor of standing before those he teaches or pastors as an "expert." Simple use of God's Word with the goal of being a doer of the Word does not bring so much honor. For when that is the standard for honor, the Holy Spirit confers it on whom he will. And it will not necessarily be the one who is greeted respectfully as "Pastor."

Overwhelmed by the "expertise" of theologians, the student or the person being confirmed or the church member loses all confidence of being able to personally understand God's Word. Another loss, typically, is the joy the Christian once had in the Bible.

Assumption and Fact

Nowhere is so much "taken on faith" as in scientific study, at least theological study. There are, of course, arguments to support the individual hypotheses. But the average, indeed even the careful student accepts 80–90 percent of the hypotheses without being in any position to evaluate the arguments. He accepts 40–50 percent of them, perhaps even more, without even knowing what the arguments are. As a rule, in teaching institutions these supporting arguments come into view only when theses are being advanced which are relatively new and not yet generally accepted, or when the teacher encounters objections to his remarks which force him to give reasons for his outlook. Careful orientation in a given area of knowledge does, to be sure, take place in individual cases, but this is not the rule, nor can it be. For the edifice of science consists of a plethora of hypotheses, each of which depends for its support on numerous arguments.

A series of basic assumptions having the character of a *consensus communis*, in that they are generally endorsed among the guild of scientists, form a grid without which it is simply impossible to grasp or process the information presented in lectures and seminars.

These basic assumptions are placed on the same level as fact, not in theory, of course, but certainly in practical application. That is, one makes use of them as if they were facts. Anyone who incorporates these basic assumptions into his thinking is influenced and ultimately changed by them.

The risk involved in critical theological study is so great because such change takes place inexorably and imperceptibly. One breathes in an atmosphere as deadly as that polluted with carbon monoxide, an odorless and colorless gas difficult to detect. No less difficult to detect are the harmful effects of critical theological study. The only hope is for God's grace to intervene in a distinct way.

The objectivity of scientific work is to a large extent illusion. In practice extra-scientific elements play a considerable role. Some examples: the formation of groups;[3] the personality and

3. [In personal correspondence Linnemann gives here the example of W. Pannenberg, T. Rendtorff, and U. Wilckens, a "group" which emerged in the early 1960s. With doctorates fresh in hand they entered the scene in tight formation as founders of a new theological direction (see Pannenberg's *Offenbarung*

public relations skill of the person advocating a given idea; the "name" of a scientist (which can have varying significance in different theological camps); whether someone holds a key position such as a professorship or is the head of an institute and, most important, whether one is an editor of a journal or the advisor to publishers regarding what gets published in monograph series.

Ostensibly, the student is in a position to form an objective opinion. In reality the intake of information is screened in advance. This screen, or filter, is formed . . .

through teachers. The student's choice of college, often based on totally different criteria than those upheld by the college chosen, can be decisive for the theological orientation he receives.

through the limitation of possibilities to study the whole range of relevant books. The student can only work through a selection and therefore holds primarily to that which is recommended in the lectures and seminars. Even the student who makes independent choices catches a glimpse of only a small part of what is available. The literature in the departmental and university libraries is screened in advance. Christian literature from Bible-believing authors is practically taboo. The productions of some publishers are not taken seriously and cannot be listed in the bibliography of a formal term paper, unless one is prepared to get a lower grade for doing so. The professor is not really familiar with these works either and feels under pressure when the student quotes them in his writing. The professor would have to get hold of, read, and interact with them. Already pressed for time and convinced from the start of

---

als Geschichte [Göttingen, 1961], ET *Revelation as History* [London, 1969]). In this way they gained an influence which they would never have had as individuals. In short order each of them occupied a university chair, which under normal conditions would have taken much longer. This is an example of "group formation," in which each individual receives the advantage of the weight of the whole group as it moves in a new direction. As soon as the three were established, the group was forgotten; each turned to other subjects. Had they each entered the scene individually, they would have been greeted with the expectation that their ideas would soon play themselves out and would never have been taken seriously, Linnemann suggests.]

the dubiousness of these publications, the professor will usually reject them.

through the student's own academic involvement. Students are offered the opportunity to "take part in scientific inquiry." A closer look, however, reveals that this involves either the taking on of time-consuming routine tasks, which the professor would like to have done in preparation for a project he is contemplating, or a study of prepackaged material. The study proceeds, then, the same way that children put together a certain house or vehicle with Lego parts. Of course variations are possible, but they turn out to be less than optimal compared with the preplanned model, as the professor or even the more advanced student can easily demonstrate. Through the material, the expected result is guaranteed; nevertheless, the student has ostensibly "convinced himself." In this fashion rebels are tamed so they fit into the system. The honor of being taken seriously as a researcher adds its weight to the attractiveness of all this.

Socialization and Conformity

The course of studies has the character of a secondary socialization. The student is profoundly affected. He takes up formal study as a rank novice, as one who knows nothing and can do nothing and is ignorant of the practices and rules of the game. In order to be accepted, he must own these practices and rules and attain the expertise and knowledge that count.

The student is inundated by a veritable flood of information which no pedagogical device is able to hold back. The professor disseminates in lectures and seminars the results of a life's work, which is based on the work of prior generations of researchers. For their part the students have trouble just comprehending the methods by which the professor's results are obtained. In view of this deluge of information it is difficult to hold onto the insights into God's Word one had at the beginning of formal study, especially when such insights are disqualified as "unscientific." The student who is a believer often encounters opposition from instructors in these forms:

Condescension: "I'm sure you'll catch on eventually!"

Temptation: "For crying out loud, accept this viewpoint at least theoretically and see how it works!"

Seduction: "Is your faith then so weak, and do you trust God so little, that you refuse to accept this idea?"

Thus is the student led personally to accept ideas that conflict with what previously was learned in God's Word.

At the same time, the student faces powerful peer pressure. Fellow students are "coinstructors," giving decisive direction in the process of socialization. This is especially true of upperclassmen, or those who have distinguished themselves by special ability or aptitude. A student who is a believer, who because of his attitude towards God's Word is unwilling to accept certain methods or results of historical criticism, is generally discriminated against. Such a student is smiled at patronizingly, mocked, and—though at times secretly respected—treated as an outsider. If he skillfully articulates a personal outlook, he may win grudging respect here and there. But he can count on full acceptance of views only on particular points, at best, and these will be points which are not too far removed from the traditionally accepted framework of the scientific discipline in question.

To the extent that the student is increasingly initiated into the historical-critical mode of thinking, he becomes alienated from those with whom he once shared close fellowship in the faith. They no longer "speak the same language," and the student has a hard time listening to them. He no longer understands them, and vice versa. Isolated, the person stands in danger of thinking himself superior and so becomes all the more susceptible to the peer pressure exerted by instructors and fellow students.

The student also must present papers which demonstrate that the approach of historical-critical theology has been sufficiently appropriated. He is compelled to think, to talk, and to write historically-critically. Apart from overt intervention of God's grace this leads to a weighty shift in thinking and in faith. The person is no longer the same, for this handling of God's Word is fundamentally transformed, even in reading for personal edification. What was learned in studies interposes itself between the Christian and the Word and bars access.

Words and Meaning

In the practical handling of the Christian tradition common to historical-critical theology, something takes place which, in the study of gnosticism, has come to be called *pseudomorphōsis.*

Pseudomorphōsis. occurs when concepts are emptied of their original meaning and then filled with a new content which has no
more in common with the original meaning than the name
itself. This confusion of meanings is encountered at every turn
in theological science. Biblical concepts such as justification by
faith, substitution, grace, redemption, freedom, original sin,
faith, prayer, and Jesus' divine sonship continue to be used, but
in such a way that they are given new and different meanings.

That Jesus is God's Son, for example, is often not taken to
mean that he is "God of God, Light of Light, Very God of Very
God." It is understood as just a cipher which expresses that
there was something special about the "historical Jesus" which
sets him apart from other great figures in history, and that in
him we are—somehow—in contact with God. In this connection
one hears the expression that every age has its own fate and
must work out its own Christology. I have heard this formula
for the last thirty years. I used to propagate it myself and with
great fervor waited for such a Christology—in vain. It turned
out that this formula was just a charter that allowed what God's
Word tells us about our Lord and Savior Jesus to be set aside as
nonbinding, as the Christology of the past

It is common to hear scholars assert that *Messiah* is just an
honorable title, as are *Son of God* and *Savior*. Such titles were
attached to Jesus by various segments of early Christianity. They
did this to express his "relevance" to those who associated their
religious hopes with such titles. Today many do not hesitate to
say that through such titles Jesus "was hyped by his follow-
ers"—he was claimed to be something he actually never was.
Anyone who adopts this manner of thinking forsakes plain faith
in God's Word and brings havoc on personal experience with
God as a result. "If you believe, you will receive," Luther stated
rightly. If I disbelieve, or believe only part of what God's Word
says about Jesus, then he will be correspondingly less to me personally. I will experience Jesus only to the level my faith allows,
and by my attitude I will lack in his blessings and his fellowship.
Let us not be dissuaded from the position that Jesus is the
Messiah, the Son of God, the Savior, even if we are accused of
using an obsolete and unsatisfactory philosophy because we, in
the view of some, accept mere words as facts.

There is just one concept dealing with salvation from the Holy
Scripture which has not been included in the above-mentioned
confusion of terms: the blood of Jesus. This has not been rede-

fined but simply rejected. It is pushed aside with the claim that talk of blood is a dubious leftover from an era in which, for both Jews and non-Jews, blood sacrifice was the order of the day.

Only the Holy Spirit can give us the light we need to see through this confusion of terms. We can ask God for the wisdom to do this. We are dealing here with a web of deception that is so finely spun and woven that we can get by it only with the help of the Holy Spirit. Let us not deceive ourselves—the theology professors believe what they say. They themselves are caught in the web, until God by grace takes them out of the domain of darkness and into the kingdom of his dear Son (Col. 1:13–14).

It is said that the old concepts, as they were originally used, are no longer accessible to modern man, and one must therefore transpose the concepts into the contemporary situation. It is demanded that there be a distinction made in God's Word between what is said and what is meant. But against these claims the Scripture asserts: "All Scripture is God-breathed and is useful for teaching, rebuking, correcting and training in righteousness, so that the man of God may be thoroughly equipped for every good work" (2 Tim. 3:16–17).

It is likewise said that Holy Scripture is both Word of God and word of man, as our Lord Jesus is God and man according to church confession. The same confession, however, asserts that these natures of Christ are "without confusion, without separation."[4] It is therefore not permissible, and also not possible, to sort out the time-conditioned human word from the eternally valid divine Word. In a mixture of iron filings and sawdust, one can use a magnet to draw out the iron. God's Word, however, is not a mixture of valid Word of God and time-conditioned word of man which can be separated from each other.

Consequences of Historical-Critical Theology

These lines are not written for the purpose of condemning persons for whom, after all, our Lord Jesus went to the cross. The purpose is rather to characterize the danger posed by the

4. [Linnemann refers to the Definition of Chalcedon (A.D. 451), in which theologians acknowledged Christ's two natures, both existing "unconfusedly, unchangeably, indivisibly, and inseparably." See "Chalcedon, Definition of (451)," in J. D. Douglas, ed., The New International Dictionary of the Christian Church (Grand Rapids: Zondervan, 1981), 209.]

system of historical-critical theology. What I have tried to do is comparable to putting an appropriate warning label on a bottle of poisonous liquid, so that no one inadvertently drinks it thinking it will be a nutritious and tasty snack.

If one realizes what critical study of theology involves, then one will no longer automatically assume that someone should *of course* study theology if he is called by God to become an apostle, a missionary, an evangelist, a pastor, or a teacher (see Eph. 4:11). In the world one must, if possible, complete a course of study in order to have a good income and "make something out of life." This world is not our home, however, but our citizenship is in heaven (Phil. 3:20). We are admonished not to be conformed to the world (Rom. 12:2). We are not to forget that the world hates us (John 15:19; 1 John 3:13). We are soldiers of Jesus Christ, and no soldier sets out without marching orders, especially not into enemy territory. If he does it anyway, he is asking for a lot of trouble.

A young person facing the question of whether to engage in critical theological study should, with a pure heart and with willingness to give up personal plans, ask God if that is his will. The individual should gain clear guidance regarding a call by the Lord, not only to become a strategic component in the body of Christ (Eph. 4:16), but also expressly to the formal study of theology.

Whomever the Lord calls to formal theological training should give himself joyously and confidently to the task as an envoy of the King, who knows how to protect his subjects even under a theology faculty. But the student must plot movements there with care, like a soldier does behind enemy lines.

Whoever has not received such a call to get formal theological training should know that many possibilities are available to our Father in heaven for preparing a person for service:

> Joseph was not trained in the royal academy of administration to be second in command over Egypt under Pharaoh, but rather in the royal dungeon.
>
> Moses, since he was regarded as a son of Pharaoh's daughter, was instructed in all the sciences and arts of the Egyptians. But what prepared him to lead his people out of Egypt into

the promised land was a forty-year education as a shepherd in the desert for his father-in-law Jethro.

Joshua received his preparation through serving as Moses' subordinate for a period of decades.

God says, "My son, give me your heart and let your eyes keep to my ways" (Prov. 23:26).

7

The Faith of Theology
and the Theology of Faith

Scientific Study

Scientific study is first of all a process by which the mind is disciplined. First, the act of thinking is detached from how it personally affects the thinker. Those questions which move the heart and occupy the mind, which bother a person and demand answers, are spurned in favor of "scientific questions." For a while the student might think that answers to the questions the person has brought to the search will come from science. In time one realizes that there are no scientific answers to "pre-scientific" questions. In the world of science such questions are not relevant anyway. Second, one's intellectual faculties are honed and polished for ready use. The student drills in observation, identification, comparison, differentiation, organization, and classification. He develops skills in the use of presuppositions, in drawing conclusions, and in much more. The result of such—at the start often arduous—exercise is personal gain. The student learns to develop ability and is set apart from those who lack such ability.

Third, the student learns to acquire a wide range of data and array them in the conceptual framework provided by the discipline in such a way that broader connections gradually become familiar. Due to the effort necessarily expended, this outcome is naturally regarded as a considerable enrichment. The student has the impression that he now has perspective, whereas in the first semesters he was groping in thick fog. Automatically a feeling of superiority develops towards those who do not (yet) share this perspective. What has been acquired is prized and valuable

104

because of the earlier humiliating situation of being lost in a forest of new ideas without knowing how to go about finding the way out. Fourth, in the advanced semesters the student learns to express this outlook amidst the plethora of divergent viewpoints and to establish a position bolstered with skillful arguments. This convinces one of intellectual sufficiency and independence. That is a highly pleasurable sensation, which compensates for some of the trouble and effort of past months and years.

Fifth, a certain percentage of students whose minds have been carefully trained reach the level of disciplined creativity which leads to new scientific knowledge.[1] This is felt by not a few people to be such a meaningful goal in life, and to be so profoundly fulfilling, that they are willing to live a truly ascetic life of sixty-hour weeks stretching over years and decades, sinking the biggest part of their assets into tools for their research in the process.

Scientific study is not only a mental training process but also a process of mental regimentation. Every scientific discipline presents a complex of traditions that has been formed through the problems that have been recognized in a particular discipline over the course of time, through the attempted solutions that have been put forth, and through the acceptance or rejection of these solutions due to the influence of scientific viewpoints as well as due to external factors that have nothing to do with science. Even when practitioners of a discipline are unconscious of the history of their subject, or just fail to take it into account, this complex of traditions regulates the entire scope of scientific work within the discipline. New scientific knowledge can only surface if it is closely linked with the complex of traditions.

The regimentation of thought that goes on in each scientific area is a learning process which leads one from being subject to the limits set by others to being subject to the limits set by oneself. In itself this regimentation of thought should not be looked on negatively, for it is a necessity if thought is to be communicable. I can entertain great ideas, but this remains a useless capacity if it never takes place on a level which enables others to participate in and make reference to my ideas.

1. Creativity as such is actually somewhat higher in the earlier semesters. I refer here to creativity which is in a position to arrive at innovative insights through consistent shaping within the complex of accepted ideas of a given scientific discipline. These insights then become components within that complex.

In theory scientific thought is autonomous and recognizes no limitation. "The independence of science" and "academic freedom" are generally recognized as justified demands. In practice this freedom exists only within the complexes of traditions which are in place in each of the various subjects and disciplines. Moreover, there exists considerable obliviousness to this state of affairs, even if the individual scientist has had painful experience with it. In scientific presentations this situation is sometimes seen when it is remarked in retrospect that the time was not yet right for a certain finding. What that actually means is that a finding had not been acceptably integrated into the complex of traditions. Thus maverick outlooks or minority viewpoints perish on the periphery, overtaken by the lava flow of the stream of tradition. Or the view is gradually adopted in a conscious bridge-building move when a marginal position comes to be shared by a large enough number of individuals.

Scientific formulation of questions does not usually originate in the object being investigated, at least not primarily, but rather in the respective givens of the complex of traditions. An autonomous science, meaning one which is subject only to the regularities of disciplined thought and obligated only to the object being researched, does not exist, at least not in the sense that an individual researcher can be autonomous. The rise of a separate complex is possible and, as far as I can see, has been partially already realized. In this case one must reckon with widespread discrimination and negation of the new formation. If, however, the new formation proves viable, there are sure to be tendencies for established positions to embrace it for integration into the complex of tradition.

From the preceding it should be clear that scientific study is not merely the collecting of useful findings or the seeking of answers to important questions. It is not merely an education in which capabilities are developed and readiness is gained. Scientific study brings about, rather, a profound alteration in the person of the one who engages in it. The training of the mind leaves an indelible mark which the student, regardless of the possible side effects, necessarily chalks up as gain. The student can likewise not avoid regimented thinking if studies are to be completed successfully. Submission is not simply an intellectual exercise; to a great extent the student is inexorably required to personalize the tradition. It is not so much that the answers are dictated; it is that the formulation of questions is determined in advance, which has the effect of preprogramming the answers that will be arrived at, even if the student arrives at them in a relatively independent fashion.

We must keep these insights before us as we now turn to the scientific theology which is taught in our universities.

The Faith of Theology

The one who takes up study is required to approach theological study "without presuppositions," to seek the truth "radically and without holding back." All that has previously been learned from God's Word and experienced in faith is to be laid aside in favor of that which must be learned in studies.

After all, the student has come to college to learn and proceeds on the assumption that in the course of studies he will penetrate deeper into the knowledge of the truth. The exacting demand to give up all former convictions thus seems bearable, though it perhaps is painful. But the student accepts it, for he is striving for the truth, and truth is promised.

What is concealed from the student is the fact that science itself, including and especially theological science, is by no means unbiased and presuppositionless. The presuppositions which determine the way work is carried on in each of its disciplines are at work behind the scenes and are not openly set forth.

The fundamental presupposition of university theology in its entirety, as it is presently espoused in our universities, is the conviction that the final authority regarding what is true is the trained, professionally informed, regimented critical intellect. That is, holy Scripture is subordinated to reason. Reason decides what in the Scripture is true and real. Reason decides what is certain, probable, or improbable in the Bible and what did not, does not, and never will occur. The critical intellect decides whether God is to be viewed as someone who acts and speaks, or whether "God" is actually simply human ideas and concepts about a hypothetical divine being.

Here reason makes use of the possibilities of knowing that are inherent to it. Critical intellect cannot conceive of a truly unique event; it must therefore assert as a fundamental presupposition the basic uniformity of all that happens and ever has happened. Critical intellect acquires knowledge only through comparison and differentiation. Where, therefore, it seeks knowledge, it must first lay out levels of comparison. Revelation is inconceivable to critical intellect; its standard is what it sees as human experience common to all men at all times. It judges by fleshly standards. It is inherently and completely unsuited to evaluate that which is spiritual—which must be evaluated spiritually. To it, the spiritual is no more than a concept, an idea with no connection to reality.

Let us illustrate this by taking an example from the Bible. For the believer John 3:16 is reality: "For God so loved the world that he gave his one and only Son, that whoever believes in him shall not perish but have eternal life." For this the Christian gives thanks to God.

As a student engaged in theological work he is to distance himself from this reality. He must instead watch how such a statement is strapped onto the procrustean bed of comparative religions analysis: Such analysis totally disregards reality and truth. What is analyzed is, from the start, reduced to thoughts, ideas, and concepts. Thoughts, ideas, and concepts from various religions are compared with one another. The question of correlation is continually posed: Can one be derived from the other, or is there a mutual influence?

For John 3:16 the result of such an approach, greatly oversimplified, might turn out something like this: *Son of God* was understood only in adoptionistic terms in Judaism, not in terms of a man having essential unity with the one true God. Further, the "sons of God" in pagan religions were not bearers of revelation from God. This leaves as comparative source material for John 3:16 only gnostic, specifically Mandean, writings. In favor of this one can point out that the bearers of revelation in these writings speak using concepts that the Jesus of John's Gospel uses (such as light-darkness and life-death). Otherwise no parallels to John can be found in these writings. The *logos* of John's Gospel is the Creator of the world; the bearers of revelation in the Mandean writings are not. They also say nothing of redemption through the cross. The temporal base line also does not work out: The Mandean writings date centuries later, which has caused some to posit the existence of an earlier Mandeanism. Now, all these discrepancies are seen, but they are not regarded as sufficient ground to call in question the comparative religions approach. The discrepancies simply furnish an extended arena for the forming of hypotheses, that is, for houses of cards made with assumptions which stand only by virtue of the support they receive from other assumptions.

If the comparative religions point of reference is not seen in the Mandean writings, but rather in those of Qumran, differences and certain shifts of emphasis emerge. The basic conception, however, remains precisely the same: John 3:16 owes its existence to connections with non-Christian religions of antiquity, whether by adopting their views or by rejecting them wholly or in part. What was originally Christian is perceived as simply an offshoot of previously established patterns. Whatever specific shape the presumed comparative religions connections take, one aspect of the method remains constant. A house of cards constructed using assumptions must be erected. The entire result is nothing but conjecture, which is made more or less plausible by means of argument.

The side benefit to all this is, of course, a considerable mental satisfaction through the intellect's validation of itself. It took hard work to sift through mutually opposed conjectures and proposed solutions and balance them off against each other. The researcher gains an impression of superiority. For he has succeeded in obliterating previous explanations of the data, which from his viewpoint were deficient, by means of a newer and more comprehensive account. He is profoundly convinced that he has rendered truth a service and contributed to the proclamation of the gospel.

Such a conviction is indisputably sincere. But such a bold undertaking has nothing to do with the way, the truth, and the life. This sort of an intellectual exercise reduces a verse such as John 3:16 to a bunch of religious ideas and theological concepts. It ceases to be God's Word that leads to salvation. The presupposition with which investigation was begun—to carry out research as if there were no God—establishes the results before observation ever begins.

It is prejudice to assert that all that can ever have happened is that which happens to every person at every time in the same way. On this basis, for example, Mark 13:2 is declared to be a *vaticinium ex eventu* ("prophecy" after the event has actually happened): It cannot be a genuine prophecy in the judgment of critical research, because exactly what it foretells came to pass. Historical-critical theology recognizes, apparently, human presentiment and foresight, so that it is conceded to Jesus that he may have been able to foresee his execution. However, there is no such thing as a knowledge of future things given by God.

One can also observe the sort of houses of cards which critical research erects by observing that the same passage, Mark 13:2, which was just arbitrarily declared to be *vaticinium ex eventu*, bears the load of proof for the assertion that Mark's Gospel arose after A. D. 70. This premise then is installed as the cornerstone for the dating of the rest of the Gospels and Acts. Truly, the historical-critical method is a colossus that stands on very shaky clay feet!

It is prejudice—not the result of scientific investigation—that one cannot, according to the historical-critical method, read the accounts of miracles in the New Testament as reports of miracles that actually took place. I myself taught often enough—as I was taught decades earlier—that self-evidently one cannot accept that these miracles took place in this way. After God through his grace convicted me that he still does such wonders even today, I began to ponder what arguments were available to support the claim that miracles cannot occur. To my shame I had to concede that there were none, for the presence of parallels in comparative religions which are sometimes used to discredit the miracles spoken of in the Bible is really no proof at all.

No argument from the Old Testament, which reports feeding miracles and resuscitations from the dead, can be used to discredit the New Testament accounts, unless one presupposes that which one seeks to prove, that the New Testament accounts are to be accounted for as literarily dependent on the Old Testament.

The largest share of the ancient healing miracles that have been collected by Weinreich tell of persons who lived long after the Gospels were written.[2] This remains true even if we accept the late dates for the Gospels proposed by the historical-critical method. In all fairness this would seem to be proof that the New Testament is influencing what happened later, rather than vice versa. It is true that miracles are reported of ancient cities like Epidaurus, which are said to have been the sites of healings. But that is also no proof that the New Testament accounts of miracles are secondary literary formations. For one thing, the findings make a literary derivation impossible. In addition, one must

---

2. Otto Weinreich, *Antike Heilungswunder* (Gießen: Töpelmann, 1909).

reckon that the sinister aspect of the unseen world may have been at work at such sites.

These are only a few suggestions. A more intensive investigation would show that underlying the historical-critical approach is a series of prejudgments which are not themselves the result of scientific investigation. They are rather dogmatic premises, statements of faith, whose foundation is the absolutizing of human reason as a controlling apparatus.

To the extent that God and Jesus Christ are spoken of based on this foundation, we are obviously dealing with syncretism—a statement for which more specific proof would have to be furnished through a more lengthy study.

The Theology of Faith

The rejection of a theology whose foundation is faith in reason by no means constitutes the absolute rejection of all theology. Nor does it constitute a rejection of the intellect in the area of theology. The Holy Spirit, like the wind, moves as he wishes, and is not dependent on the presupposition of an academically disciplined intellect. He can cause cooks, bakers, cobblers, and factory workers to be powerful preachers of the gospel. Academic education is no guarantee of possessing the Holy Spirit's power. However, the disciplined intellect can be used by the Holy Spirit and become a precision tool in the Spirit's hand, when and where God sees fit.

In the theology of faith, the necessary regulation of thought must occur through the Holy Scripture. It controls the thought process. Thought must subordinate itself to the Word of God. If difficulties crop up, it does not doubt God's Word but its own wisdom. It asks God for wisdom in the expectation that it will receive what it has requested, waiting patiently for God's timing. It presupposes the truth and the unity of God's Word and is for that reason in a position to recognize and experience that truth and unity in a very real way. It believes the Scripture, which says of itself that it is divinely given. It is mindful that Jesus Christ has become for us wisdom (1 Cor. 1:30), and that because of this a distinction must be made between divine wisdom and that wisdom which is "earthly, unspiritual, of the devil" (James 3:15).

Thought which allows regulation by the holy Scripture

refrains from pointless controversies and rationalistic quests for novelty. It allows its thoughts to be taken captive under God's Word (see 2 Cor. 10:5). It is not interested in playing such games as "But what about if . . . ?" "But couldn't we also assume . . . ?" Holy Scripture is, after all, the Father's Word to us. The way we treat it is the way we encounter our Father in heaven.

Questions are solved on one's knees, not through ransacking commentaries. God can, it is true, use the work of brothers who have written commentaries to instruct us, and we are grateful for their counsel. But they are helpful only under God's direction, and we are relying on flesh if we depend on them alone to strengthen our hands.

The fruit of theological study conducted under the auspices of the theology of faith ought to include a thorough mastery of grammar and lexicography, the ability to read God's Word profitably in the original languages and to check translations.

Fruitful study should check and incorporate the stock of available background information regarding peoples and kings mentioned in the Old and New Testaments, geography and climate, the existence and impact of civil laws, and other factors. It should draw from a broad awareness of God's saving plan and be in a position to share the whole counsel of God—able to correctly handle the Word of truth (2 Tim. 2:15), to uphold the Word in keeping with sound doctrine, and to admonish with sound teaching and to convict those who contradict, defending the most holy faith (Titus 1:9).

Relationships and connections in God's Word should be studied to discern, for example, how the laws of sacrifice foreshadowed Jesus' saving work, or how the prophecy in Revelation was already disclosed a portion at a time by the Old Testament prophets. There should be the discovery that God's Word yields hidden treasures to humble searching, such as the foreshadowing references to Jesus in the tabernacle, or how the genealogies contribute in their own way to the exaltation of God.

There also, however, needs to be the ability to distinguish between genuine treasures and eccentric trivialities. Intellectual pleasure is a fact of life. God can use it, but when the flesh takes hold of it—and the flesh is ever ready to rear its ugly head—then emphasis is not given to the hidden treasures of God's Word, shown by its divine author. Rather, the Word becomes a quarry for erratic discoveries, and entire theologies are built on some dependent clause in the Bible.[3] What is truly lamentable is that an author can honestly suppose that insights were given through the Holy Spirit. That is the way we are, and for that reason we need correction from each other as Christians. Anybody who thinks he would rather just trust his own intellect will not avoid error by that strategy: "We all stumble in many ways" (James 3:2).

Solid knowledge of the Word of God as just described can be used by God to unmask theologies based on eccentric discoveries and aberrant theologies.[4] But note carefully: I said "used by God." The theologian does not, by virtue of his academic study, occupy the judge's bench. God alone is right.

When *we* think that we are right, we may find ourselves in a situation like that described in Judges 20:12–28: Because of a despicable crime that had been committed in Gibeah, eleven tribes of Israel came out to oppose the twelfth, the tribe of Benjamin, because it was not willing to hand over the perpetrators of the crime. The reason they had taken up arms was truly legitimate, and they had also inquired of the Lord, whether they should go out for battle. Nevertheless, the Lord twice allowed the eleven tribes to be battered by the one—presumably because in their hearts they were looking at the matter as their business, as their expression of righteous indignation, rather than as the Lord's affair. When, finally, at the third attack the Lord gave Benjamin into their hands, they fought with such abandon that they forgot that they were fighting some of God's own people. The tribe of Benjamin was nearly annihilated, and since Israel could only appear before the Lord with all the tribes represented, the problem had to be solved of how this tribe could be saved from dying out, since only six hundred young men and no women at all had survived.

It is not we who need to swing into action at our discretion; it is rather God using us as instruments, if he so wishes. Then it is our job to obey.

3. [In personal correspondence Linnemann makes it clear that she is *not* saying here that some parts of Scripture, for example dependent clauses, are less important than others. She gives as an example of the error she has in mind the way some use 3 John 2. Here John writes: "Dear friend, I pray that you may enjoy good health and that all may go well with you even as your soul is getting along well." When someone deduces from this that a Christian need never be sick and that it is always God's will for a Christian to enjoy perfect health, a theology has been wrongly built on inadequate footings, according to Linnemann.]

4. Such as those referred to in the previous note.

8

The Mentality
of Historical-Critical Theology

An example will illustrate the way that historical-critical theology characteristically thinks and operates. It is my intention to show what normally and commonly occurs. Therefore, I have chosen a section from a book that is written for a broad circle of readers, including nontheologians. The author of this book is a renowned theologian and prolific scholar who tends to be conservative rather than critical. This choice of subject was carefully made to better justify the generalizations we will base on our observations.

In his *The Theology of the New Testament*, Werner Georg Kümmel states that "in the second half of the eighteenth century, in connection with the intellectual movement of the Enlightenment, within Protestant theology the insight began to prevail that the Bible is a book written by men, which, like any product of the human mind, can properly be made understandable only from the times in which it appeared and therefore only with the methods of historical science."[1]

This statement misleads the impartial reader into assuming that he must accept as fact that the Bible is only a product of the human mind. The basic premise of historical-critical theology—that the Bible is to be viewed as a creation of the human mind and cannot be handled any differently than other products of human mental activity—is presented to the reader as *established fact* (or "insight" by Kümmel). That is, the statement appears to be an insight based on familiarity with certain

1. (Nashville: Abingdon, 1973), 14.

given facts. Inevitably the reader will regard this so-called knowledge as a result of research that has gained dominance and general recognition. A layperson who is not aware of all the facts will accept the premise because the entire authority of science stands behind it. This insight, this established fact, it appears, gained acceptance in science centuries ago.

In this way a person gets caught in the web of deception. The so-called knowledge was in truth only a decision. A tiny minority among members of the elite Western intellectuals, decided to regard man as the measure of all things (humanism). Consequently, they recognized as truth only that which they could arrive at inductively (Enlightenment, Francis Bacon). That was the decision to suppress the truth in unrighteousness. Thus men rejected God's Word as revealed truth and opted for the wisdom of this world, which is essentially atheistic, even if it pretends to be devout and mouths the name of God. The decision to suppress the truth in unrighteousness, which at first was made by only a few who fancied themselves to be wise, has in the meantime gained such prominence that today in Germany even children, right down to the last grade school student, are indoctrinated with this view.

Another glance at Kümmel will help us understand how such views spread as they do: One alleges—as already stated—to have a basis of solid knowledge, undergirded by facts and the truth, on which to stand. Based on this, one argues that the consequences are inescapable: Because the Bible is "a product of the human mind," it "can properly be made understandable . . . only with the methods of historical science."

That sort of demagogical chicanery is probably the basic structure, not only of historical-critical theology, but also of a whole range of disciplines in the humanities. The language of this demagogery begins:

"As anyone can see . . .";

"Everyone must recognize . . .";

"The conclusion is inescapable . . .";

"The assumption is compelling . . .";

"One must not overlook that . . .";

"One must. . .";

"One may not . . .";

"One cannot stop half-way . . .".

Whenever you encounter these kinds of formulations, you usually have the clay feet of the colossus *Science* before you.

Whoever maintains that the Bible can only be made understandable with the methods of critical historiography is putting a thoroughly atheistically conceived science in charge of the treasures of divine revelation. God's Word says to us that God controls the destinies of the nations; critical historiography refuses from the very start even to consider the possibility that God has worked in actual history. And then this atheistic, anti-Christian science is recognized by historical-critical theology as furnishing the only proper access to God's Word, so everyone who wishes to be regarded as theologically educated should endorse this outlook.

In order to receive an academic degree as an expert in things relating to God, I must, therefore, make the decision to make room in my thinking for atheism. I will be kindly permitted to retain my pious feelings, but my thinking must follow the pattern of the atheistic guiding principle: *ut si Deus non daretur* (as if there were no God). That is perversion!

Both historical-critical theology and critical historiography have their basis in deception. Science is, accordingly, not the synonym for truth but rather for rebellion against God which suppresses the truth in unrighteousness. The individual data which it unearths are marred and distorted, like a spoon's appearance is optically distorted in a glass of water.

Kümmel continues: "That is to say, from this insight there resulted the unavoidable conclusion that even the presentation of the thought content of the Bible, i.e. a 'Biblical Theology,' could properly occur only with the aid of historical inquiry if the thought content were to be uninfluenced by dogmatics and actually be recognized independently."[2]

Kümmel thereby assumes that I can read the Bible "uninfluenced by dogmatics" only with the help of critical historiography. In other words, I am influenced by dogmatics if I refuse to squeeze my thinking through the needle's eye of critical historiography and just read the Bible as it stands. Either I read the

2. Ibid. 14f.

Bible influenced by dogmatics—and that is improper; the Bible is then not "actually recognized independently"—or I read the Bible by means of the historical manner of formulating questions. That is proper and results in the thought content of the Bible being "*actually* recognized *independently*."[3]

The goal, then, is "actual independent recognition," in which the measure of all things is man. Atheistic critical historiography furnishes the Archemedian point[4] needed to make use of God's Word without having to get into God's Word. This seizure of the Bible from the outside reduces it to "thought content," and the result is called "theology," which is traditionally defined as "talk about God"! The perversion is monstrous! God's revelation should be "properly" and "actually independently" recognized in such a way that God is no longer spoken of, so that God is no longer honored and thanked. We have put generation after generation of believing Christian young people, who were willing and eager to serve God, through this fire, sacrificing them to the Moloch of an atheistic theology. The result has been generation after generation of misguided guides. When will we finally reverse course and renounce this idol worship?

Kümmel continues his presentation, observing what historical-critical theology feels compelled to accept after it has "investigated the Bible historically as the product of human authors": "But as soon as people actually became serious with such historical inquiry with respect to the ideas of the Bible, as first happened around 1800, they found themselves compelled not only completely to separate the presentation of the Old and New Testaments from each other, but also, in the portrayal of the ideas of the New Testament, to let Jesus and the various apostolic authors speak each for himself."[5]

His speech betrays him, or rather, betrays historical-critical theology, which Kümmel represents: "they found themselves compelled not only . . . but also . . .". Whoever ventures into this mode of godlessness is from then on not able to make independent decisions; something or someone is there to compel. That is honestly stated. This compulsion is not exerted through

3. [Linnemann's emphasis.]

4. [Linnemann literally writes Archimedes' words, *pou stoo* or "where to stand," a reference to his remark that if he were furnished a firm place to stand outside the earth, he could move it.]

5. Kümmel, *Theology of the New Testament*, 15.

rules of logic or tried-and-true methods; these will not coerce.
We are dealing with demonic forces, under whose sway one falls
when one starts down this path. One is no longer free but is
under a spell.

Based on what we have already quoted, Kümmel draws this
conclusion:

> One simply could not stop halfway; if the Bible must be histor-
> ically investigated as the work of human authors in order to
> understand its actual meaning, then one may not and cannot
> cling to the assumption that the Old Testament and New
> Testament form, each in itself, a conceptual unity, and then one
> must also heed the differences *within* the two Testaments and also
> take into consideration a possible development and adulteration
> of the ideas. Consequently the concern about a theology of the
> New Testament found itself from the outset confronted with the
> problem of diversity and unity in the New Testament.[6]

It is outrageous, but there it stands: "The Bible must be historically investigated as the work of human authors in order to
understand its actual meaning." That is not first demonstrated; it
is, rather, presupposed from the outset. And that is not the private opinion of Kümmel; it is, rather, the common assumption
of historical-critical theology, which I mention once again here
to indicate the consequences of adopting it. The consequence is
the atomization of the Bible: One ends up holding pieces without recognizing the living context. In a helplessness which is
one's own fault, one finally goes so far as to regard the Bible's
statements as quite possibly an "adulteration" of ideas.

That is how the holy Scripture of the holy God is treated! The
Word of our Redeemer is thus trampled underfoot. Then on the
mission field, Moslems confront the missionaries with choice
excerpts from the works of historical-critical theologians and
declare, "Your own people say that the Bible is not true!" Truly,
God is longsuffering and patient. But make no mistake; he will
not be mocked. Judgment is coming. Blessed is the one who has
taken refuge in the blood of Jesus!

Kümmel continues:

> Therefore from the very beginning the concern with the theo-
> logical content of the New Testament as an independent histori-

6. Ibid. [Emphasis in this and succeeding quotations is Kümmel's.]

cal entity stood in tension with every form of dogmatic theology. For the presentation of Christian doctrine as answer to the question about the essence of God's revelation in Jesus Christ, from whatever presuppositions it proceeds and whatever connections are placed upon it, obviously must have the aim of setting forth a *unified* teaching. Therefore dogmatics must fall into difficulties when it seeks to find support in the New Testament as the basis of its utterances and finds that biblical theology is unable to exhibit any unitary teaching in the New Testament to that end. Here the actual problem of a "theology of the New Testament" confronts us.[7]

This passage affords especially clear insight into how Kümmel's approach works:

Through the introduction of the concept *tension* ("stood in tension"), the investigation is from the start catapulted out of the realm of the two coordinates *truth* and *lie*.

Dogmatic theology is introduced as the standard of comparison. That is, objections based on a faithful reading of Scripture which arise against the sort of New Testament theology Kümmel proposes are discriminated against. They are not permitted to cross-examine in any meaningful way the assumptions of historical-critical theology. They are, rather, pushed aside as originating from the viewpoint of another subject which, just like itself, amounts to a merely human conception. This form of argumentation is not new, but that does not make it any better.

Dogmatics, seen as an opponent, is disqualified from the start as a legitimate point of view for science: Dogmatics proceeds from certain presuppositions; it has placed restrictions on itself; it is finally—despite all its admitted possible internal differences—biased in the direction of showing unity in its presuppositions and restrictions. To the extent that it stands in contrast to New Testament theology, its position is looked upon as tendentious. In this manner historical-critical theology seals itself off from discomfiting questions from the start.

The above-mentioned difficulty of Kümmel is only one of many. He does not shrink from stating: "For even if the expositor first of all concerns himself with the meaning of the *individual* writings of the New Testament . . . he is faced in principle with an insoluble task."[8] Kümmel maintains, then, clearly and

7. Ibid.
8. Ibid.

unambiguously, that the meaning of God's Word, given for our salvation, is from his standpoint beyond our grasp. Actually, such bankruptcy in interpreting the Bible should have brought into question the underlying principles of such interpretation. Instead, Kümmel proceeds as follows: "The writings collected in the New Testament are, according to their historical character, documents of ancient religious history, written in a dead language and a set of concepts and a conceptual world no longer immediately comprehensible to us. Therefore they can be made to speak only by way of historical research, and only by this way can an understanding of what was meant by the authors be approximated."[9]

It is outrageous! The book of the new covenant, which speaks of our redemption—is made a collection of "documents of ancient religious history"! "For God so loved the world, that he gave his one and only son, that whoever believes in him shall not perish . . ."—a sentence out of the documents of ancient religious history! "I am the way and the truth and the life"—the Word of our Lord and Savior—this is an aphorism from ancient religious history! "Salvation is found in no one else, for there is no other name under heaven given to men by which we must be saved"—likewise a fragment of a document from ancient religious history!

According to Kümmel, such ancient documents were "written in a dead language and a set of concepts and a conceptual world no longer immediately comprehensible to us." This is nothing less than a forceful attempt to relegate God's Word to a historical "back then," to withdraw it from use, and to make it into a museum through which tours are occasionally conducted.

Today millions of God's children experience daily the New Testament, in fact the entire Bible, as God's living Word, through which God speaks to them. Oblivious to such worldwide experiences, Kümmel maintains: "The writings collected in the New Testament . . . can be made to speak only by way of historical research." The Holy Spirit is thereby denied and Jesus contradicted, the same Jesus who stated: "I praise you, Father, Lord of heaven and earth, because you have hidden these things from the wise and learned, and revealed them to little children. Yes, Father, for this was your good pleasure" (Matt. 11:25–26). Doesn't Jesus' pronouncement of woe (Matt. 23:13) apply to

9. Ibid.

such a theology? "Woe to you, *teachers of the law and Pharisees,* you hypocrites! You shut the kingdom of heaven in men's faces. You yourselves do not enter, nor will you let those enter who are trying to."

We need to keep in view that we are not criminal detectives working on "The Kümmel Case." Werner Georg Kümmel's remarks serve merely as an example, and he is, I remind you, a moderate advocate of this theology which has spread around the world. Kümmel leaves us in absolutely no doubt as to the questionable nature of the results of critical efforts to allow the writings of the New Testament to speak by way of historical research: "Such a concern for scientific explanation by its very nature always can lead only to probable and often only to hypothetical results, and it requires the adventuresome *judgment* whether one will follow an achieved result or will replace it with another attempt at explanation."[10]

Because one has decided that the thought content of the Bible should actually be recognized independently, the unity of the Bible is dissolved and God's Word can no longer serve as its own interpreter. Consequently it is necessary to indulge in assumptions rather than to recognize facts, to connect hypotheses to other hypotheses until an entire house of cards is constructed using hypotheses.

The decisive factor in the assessing and ordering of these hypotheses is the autonomous "I," which judges God's Word according to its own discretion. The interpreter gets what he chooses; the "I" sits on the throne. In the ancient fable, King Midas could only think of gold and as a result wasted away with hunger, because in keeping with his greedy desire, everything he touched turned to gold. In the same way, that person who, in opposition to God's Word, decides for his own radical autonomy is delivered over to himself and as a result actually perceives only projections of himself. For that person God's Word really does become a dead letter. That is God's judgment!

But now the same writings of the New Testament have been collected by the early church into a canon of sacred scriptures, whose extent was no longer seriously disputed after the end of the fourth century. They have thereby acquired the character of normative writings, foundational for the faith of the Christians, to

10. Ibid. 15f.

which the Christian has to respond with believing obedience. But it is easy to see that it is basically impossible to confront the writings of the New Testament as a man making judgments in research and at the same time as one who hears in faith."[11]

That is the truth! I am not aware that any other historical-critical theologian has seen the facts with as much clarity. One would think that surely here Kümmel would call his historical-critical position into question. If it leads to such consequences, then it must be wrong-headed. But that is not what he does. Instead, he takes a final breakneck leap:

> Hence when attempts understandably have repeatedly been made in various ways to escape this dilemma, all such attempts yet were and are doomed to failure because they do not correspond to the state of things. The scientific concern with the understanding of the New Testament must, precisely when it is pursued in the context of the church and from the presupposition of faith, take account of the fact that we also *can* come to a believing hearing of the message of the New Testament only in *one* way: namely, by seeking to make the utterances of the ancient authors of the New Testament understandable, just as their contemporary readers or hearers could and had to understand them.[12]

We can agree with Kümmel that compromise solutions will not bear heavy loads. But that by no means justifies his groundless contention that it is a *fact* that believing reception of the New Testament message can occur only through the hearing aid of historical-critical theology. The smallest and youngest child of God can convict him of error in his shameless claim.

But Kümmel subsequently sets forth the thesis once more: "Hence there is no other access to the understanding of the New Testament writings than the method of historical research, which is valid for *all* writings of antiquity."[13]

The radically autonomous "I" dictates which of historical research's hypothetical results should serve as the explanation for a given passage. This process is the only access "to a believing hearing [*zum gläubigen Hören*] of the message of the New

11. Ibid. 16.
12. Ibid.
13. Ibid.

Testament." Note carefully that Kümmel writes of *gläubiges Hören* ("believing hearing") rather than *glaubendes Hören* ("faithful hearing"). *Gläubig* ("believing") connotes a subjective attribute, while *Glaube* ("faith," which would produce faithful hearing) clings trustingly to the objectively given promise.

Now Kümmel does attempt (although it is hard to see how, given his previous statements) to maintain the importance of faith in dealing with the Bible: "Of course a great deal depends on whether one pursues such research as one uninvolved and in conscious detachment, or as one inwardly involved and hence as one who hears with ultimate openness."[14]

Nevertheless, he stands by his contention that "there is no other access to the understanding of the New Testament writings." He continues, "Thus, while one who inquires after the thought content and the address of a New Testament writing sees himself confronted by the necessity of achieving a personal hearing of it by the involved route of the scientific explanation of the ancient text, this difficulty is shown in increased measure in the concern with the theology of the New Testament."[15]

"No other access"?—woe to anyone who has to stand before God's judgment seat with such a claim! I am so grateful that Jesus' blood has washed away my errors! I was no better; in fact I was worse, and I likewise made such irresponsible statements. And whoever gets involved in historical-critical theology will end up in a similar situation. One can no more be a *little* historical-critical than a *little* pregnant.

14. Ibid.
15. Ibid.

Counsel False and True

Is Your Faith Too Limited?

Sometimes children of God recoil from critical study of theology in a university because they know in their hearts that it is not the voice of the Good Shepherd that they will hear in historical-critical theology. Such believers often must face the objection: "Is then your faith so limited that you do not want to accept historical-critical theology?" That is a misleading question.

God does not demand that we put our faith to the test. We have already gone astray when we entertain the idea that our faith is at our disposal in this manner. Jesus is the author and the perfecter of our faith (Heb. 12:2), and the amount of faith we have is what God has given us (Rom. 12:3).

None of the seducers who encourage God's children to dedicate themselves to study at a place where their hearts will be defiled through long-term intellectual poisoning would be willing to allow their own bodies to be exposed to small, but in the long-run fatal, doses of arsenic. There is no way they would test their own faith and God's protection in such a manner by calling on Mark 16:18. May God grant them grace to repent, so that they cease misleading the souls entrusted to them by requiring that they place themselves in a dependent position within an atheistic, anti-Christian teaching system which works from the presupposition that there is no God.

Historical-critical theology is heresy. There is widespread agreement on this regarding Rudolf Bultmann, at least in evangelical circles. There are, however, no fundamental differences between Bultmann and the other advocates of this approach; any differences which might be discernible are at best minimal.[1] God's Word has given us clear directives as to how we are to regard heresies (2 John 10f., Rom. 16:17, Jude 23, Col. 2:8, 2 Peter 3:17, to name a few). Honoring these instructions may well be incompatible with the study of historical-critical theology.

When I, without God's leading and without being forced, enter a situation which requires that I disobey clear directives from God's Word, I cannot count on the protection God normally extends. I must rather realize that he will at least partially withdraw his protection. For this reason one must resist being misled in this matter.

Has Not God Saved People Out of Historical-Critical Theology?

The first deception is sometimes supplemented by a second. Examples are cited which show that God has saved individuals out of historical-critical theology. This is supposed to prove that the danger is not really so great, after all, when one studies this theology.

It is true that God saves some out of historical-critical theology. We thank him for this. God *can* do it. But should we for that reason expose ourselves to such danger? The devil said to Jesus, after placing him on the pinnacle of the temple: "If you are the son of God, throw yourself down. For it is written: 'He will command his angels concerning you, and they will lift you up in their hands, so that you will not strike your foot against a stone.'" But Jesus, who certainly knew that God *could* preserve him, did not venture into danger, but replied to the tempter: "It is also written: 'Do not put the Lord your God to the test'" (Matt. 4:6–7). To commit oneself to the study of historical-critical theology without clear leading from God, on the assumption that God can keep from harm, is putting God to the test.

---

1. Anyone in doubt on this point may consult the detailed evidence advanced by Ernst Bartels: *Beitrag zur Auseinandersetzung mit der Theologie von Landesbischof D. Eduard Lohse* (1984, available from the author at Breslauer Straße 10, 3429 Bilshausen). Since Lohse is one of the comparatively moderate representatives of this approach, the evidence Bartels advances is widely applicable.

Do You Want to Serve in a Mainline Church?

It is argued that a young person who wishes to study theology in order to serve God is indeed forced to attend university, at least if he wants to serve in a mainline church. Here the facts are being trusted rather than God, who knows what the facts are and can alter the circumstances. As long as the majority of students attend university and refuses to take the risk of finding no place of service in the mainline church, perhaps he will permit these circumstances to persist. If his children would perceive, however, that such study, while it assures them a place of service, makes them unfit for serving the Lord, and if they would with one voice cry out to God, asking that he break the educational monopoly of historical-critical theology, then our Father in heaven will certainly respond to the cries of his children. In his grace he has already granted us a few educational centers that are true to the Bible, and those who have attended these institutes have not remained unemployed in his kingdom.

Should You Not Follow Paul's Example?

A further deception—one which stoops to misusing God's Word—runs like this: "Paul became a Jew to the Jews and a Greek to Greeks; so let us become historical-critical to those who are historical-critical!"

God's Word is being cited here only partially, because that is the only way it can be used to support this deception. It is advisable to take note of all of 1 Corinthians 9:20–21: "To the Jews I became like a Jew, to win the Jews. To those under the law I became like one under the law (though I myself am not under the law), so as to win those under the law. To those not having the law I became like one not having the law (though I am not free from God's law but under Christ's law), so as to win those not having the law."

Paul was *like* someone under the law, although he himself was not under the law. Galatians 2:1–9 and Philippians 3:2, as well as Romans chapters 1–4 show, among other things, how this being a Jew to the Jews looks in practical terms. As a rule, however, the student is in absolutely no position to conduct himself in this way due to his internal and external dependence as one who is in training. Even Paul required a long time in preparation for the role he eventually filled. In addition, that is by no means the task of everyone who must prepare for his future service as shepherd, evangelist, and teacher.

Without a special enabling from God, promised to him through a special word from God, the student does not become like a historical-critical theologian to the historical-critical theologians as Paul became like a Jew to the Jews, according to 1 Corinthians 9:20. Instead, the student simply *becomes* a historical-critical theologian—possibly with a few cosmetic differences. However, the consequence of these differences is not missionary power; they are perceived by historical-critical theologians simply as inconsistencies. They are smiled at condescendingly or, as the case may be, endured only when the historical-critical approach applies in all other respects.

Paul did not become "a Jew to the Jews" in rabbinic study, as a member of the Sanhedrin, as an ordained rabbi nor as a coworker in a synagogue. Nor did he do so during his education. He achieved this rather as a tried and proven Christian working independently, who initiated his contacts from place to place in the synagogue but who could leave the synagogue at any time. Under this condition he could, on the basis of their own presuppositions, indicate to the Jews the necessity of a radical change of direction. He could show them their need to accept the redemption Jesus brought about on Golgotha.

Are Not All Things Yours?

Another line from Scripture that is torn from its context is "All things are yours" (1 Cor. 3:21), which is used to prove the assertion: "In the freedom of faith in Christ, disputation with any hypothesis is possible, including a historical-critical one. An anxious attitude should be overcome."[2]

It is technically true that historical-critical hypotheses can be grouped under the headings "world or life" and "the present" in the following quotation, but one must not ignore the context of the verse:

> Do not deceive yourselves. If any one of you thinks he is wise by the standards of this age, he should become a "fool" so that he may become wise. For the wisdom of this world is foolishness in God's sight. As it is written: "He catches the wise in their crafti-

2. I forego specifying the source of this quote out of consideration for the Christian brother who wrote it.

ness"; and again, "The Lord knows that the thoughts of the wise are futile." So then, no more boasting about men! All things are yours, whether Paul or Apollos or Cephas or the world or life or death or the present or the future—all are yours, and you are of Christ, and Christ is of God. [1 Cor. 3:18–23]

Historical-critical theology is "wisdom of the world," and the reputation of scientists is established through hypotheses so that these scientists receive praise and so that many will join their "school." However, we are admonished to become a "fool" so that we "may become wise" rather than to use the wisdom of the world in the freedom of Christ.

I might remark in passing: Disputation with hypotheses—to the extent that the goal is not to repudiate them through God's Word—is nothing other than playing the game of hypothesis-spinning. Such disputation places itself from the start on the ground on which those sorts of hypotheses are formed, and it has already deserted the solid basis of God's Word. In addition, it in no way eliminates the influence of such hypotheses; it rather ultimately contributes to their stabilization.

Yes, That's What the Scripture Says, But . . .

It is pernicious to handle Scripture, as some do, with the assumption that what it plainly says should be laid aside in favor of some novel theory giving a new and different sense to the words. When I approach God's Word with this attitude, I am already off course, even if the result is positive. I have placed my trust in my intellect and believed myself capable of discerning what is correct.

The appropriate attitude would be: "Father, I thank you for your Word. It is true from start to finish. Still, I have problems. I have let myself be disconcerted. When I was driven into a corner, I did not trust your Word. Please, set me straight, and show me through the Holy Spirit from your Word how things are."

The temptation is to want to stand as conqueror through the power of one's intellect and the strength of one's arguments. But God says, "Not by might, nor by power, but by my Spirit" (Zech. 4:6).

Are You Better Than These Theologians?

The really low blow among all these deceptions is the question: "Do you think that you're better . . . ?" God's Word tells us, "Count yourselves dead to sin" (Rom. 6:11). It is not demanded from us that we identify with others to the extent that we identify with their sin. I am no better than a thief, a prostitute, an adulterer, or a historical-critical theologian. But in the same way that I resist adultery in the name of Jesus, I can also resist historical-critical theology, and appeal to my Savior in time of need.

The reader who has followed the arguments of this chapter will see that the following passages provide a relevant summary:

"All the words of my mouth are just; none of them is crooked or perverse. To the discerning all of them are right; they are faultless to those who have knowledge" (Prov. 8:8–9).

"The fear of the LORD is the beginning of wisdom, and knowledge of the Holy One is understanding" (Prov. 9:10).

"The mouth of the righteous brings forth wisdom, but a perverse tongue will be cut out" (Prov. 10:31).

"Stop listening, my son, to instruction that departs from the words of knowledge" (Prov. 19:27).[3]

"He who leads the upright along an evil path will fall into his own trap, but the blameless will receive a good inheritance" (Prov. 28:10).

"Woe to those who are wise in their own eyes and clever in their own sight" (Isa. 5:21).

"This is what the LORD says: 'Cursed is the one who trusts in man, who depends on flesh for his strength and whose heart turns away from the LORD'" (Jer. 17:5).

"How can you believe if you accept praise from one another, yet make no effort to obtain the praise that comes from the only God?" (John 5:44).

"Therefore, I urge you, brothers, in view of God's mercy, to offer your bodies as living sacrifices, holy and pleasing to God—this is your spiritual act of worship. Do not conform any longer to the pattern of this world, but be transformed by the renewing of your mind. Then you will be able to test and approve what God's will is—his good, pleasing and perfect will" (Rom. 12:1–2).

---

3. [Translation follows Linnemann's rendering of the Hebrew.]

9

Historical-Critical Theology and Evangelical Theology

The Structure of Science

Science as such is a bewitching system of self-realization and reciprocal confirmation. This state of affairs is clearly demonstrated by Samuel R. Külling in his German work, which maybe translated, *On the Dating of the 'P' Source in Genesis.*[1]

The late-dating of the so-called priestly writing is, in the words of the theory's mastermind, E. Reuss (1804–91), "the product of intuition."[2] Reuss passes this intuition on immediately to his students in the easily remembered statement: "The prophets are earlier than the law, and the Psalms more recent than both."[3]

Before there was even an attempt to furnish proof, a student of Reuss named K. H. Graf (1815–69) internalizes this formula, which from then on determines his view of the history of Israel.[4] That occurs, by no means, through an arcane detail of scientific work, but through a revolutionary overturning of formerly-held viewpoints. At stake here was the question, in Reuss' own words, "whether we ought to view the history of Israel as standing on its feet or on its head."[5] Warned in advance by his teacher of the magnitude of this "finding," the student Graf at first places

1. Samuel R. Külling, *Zur Datierung der 'Genesis-P-Stücke'* (2d ed., Riehen, 1985).
2. Ibid., 5.
3. Ibid.
4. Ibid., 5; see also, 7.
5. Ibid., 5.

it on the back burner. Nevertheless, without being expressly propagated, its effects are perceptible as a background assumption in the books he authors.[6]

Although there had not even been an attempt at furnishing scientific proof—and even Reuss, the teacher, was content to make vague suggestions to avoid difficulties—the student Graf writes to Reuss, "I am totally convinced that the entire middle portion of the Pentateuch is post-exilic. . . ."[7] Being "totally convinced" is quite common in the area of "scientific" work and requires no proof. It draws from entirely different sources.

This is clearly seen in Graf's case: a review and an article which attempt to question his position serve only to confirm him all the more in his views. This confirmation comes, not through objective disputation in which he weighs opposing arguments, but through a decision.[8]

The finding that was passed from teacher to student is then interwoven with the views of colleagues and thereby gains a broader basis.[9] Various methodological starting points are employed, and the basic idea takes shape in varying clusters of questions. A process of reciprocal corroboration sets in, and a coalition forms composed of those who support the basic idea with their own thoughts. Even criticism no longer succeeds in hindering the process that is now in motion.[10]

What is striking in this process is the absence of proof. Külling states, "In the history we have sketched of the exilic/post-exilic dating of the 'P' source in Genesis, we seek in vain for arguments supporting its late dating. In 1869, the 'P' portions were assigned to the exilic/post-exilic era with one fell swoop based on literary analytical grounds."[11]

Not until later are arguments brought out to undergird the thesis, and then they do not deserve to be called "arguments," for they consist entirely of unproven assertions and judgments based on personal taste.[12]

The movement set in motion by Reuss' "intuition" regarding

6. Ibid., 7.
7. Ibid.
8. Ibid., 11.
9. Cf. ibid., 10ff. regarding Graf and Kuenen; 11ff. and 21–42 regarding Graf and Hupfeld.
10. Ibid., 36f.
11. Ibid., 43.
12. Ibid., 44–57.

the dating of the books of the Old Testament finally came to rest
when this "intuition" became part of Wellhausen's conception of
the history of Israel in his now-famous *Prolegomena to the History
of Ancient Israel* (1878). Concerning this book Külling writes:

> "The appeal of an entirely new overall picture [of Israel's his-
> tory], which this work contains, lent to that hypothesis an impor-
> tance that was instantly almost overwhelming"[. . .] . Wellhausen's
> historical reconstruction forms the crown of the assignment of a
> post-exilic origin to "P." Wellhausen presents here the conse-
> quences of this post-exilic dating of "P" for the interpretation of
> the Old Testament in its entirety. [. . .]
>
> Even if we find here no essentially new arguments for the
> post-exilic dating of "P," it is still true that Wellhausen gains a
> great number of adherents who from now on regard "P" as the
> latest of the sources[. . .] . He does this through his "masterful
> connecting of various preliminary studies to form a brilliant and
> self-contained overall picture."[. . .][13]

At the outset there was the intuition, at the end the conception, and the tradition followed; the student has to learn the
conception by heart as a "scientific result." On this he has to
build, and with it he must work. In the process that leads from
intuition to conception, argumentation also has a place.
However, it never serves to furnish proof in the strict sense;
important decisions are settled apart from argumentation.

There remains a limited place for renewed argumentation as
the tradition is carried forward. This argumentation may in
some cases even result in certain corrections. However, these
corrections can no longer call the fundamental conception into
question. For the conception, to the extent that it is has been
accepted, is built into the entire structure of the scientific discipline. Argumentation has only the character of making minor
adjustments in the course leading to the final destination of "scientific progress." This destination in itself leads to further
strengthening of the conception. [This process of taking intuition toward tradition and incorporating it into the discipline is
illustrated in figs. 9.1 and 9.2.]

A few conceptions arise independently. Most, however, build
on others and are supported, entirely or in part, by earlier ones.
Several are constructed to stabilize fringe conceptions. Others

13. Ibid., 57.

Fig. 9.1 From Intuition to Conception and Tradition

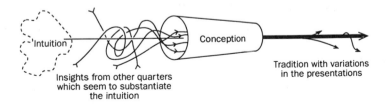

Fig. 9.2 The Rise of a Scientific Discipline: A Rough Sketch

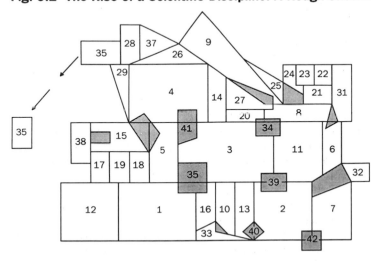

The numbered areas present conceptions in the order of their development. An exact depiction would also have presented how they dovetail. Shaded areas designate conceptions that arise in the course of correcting earlier ideas.

serve to plug gaps. Still others lead further or make corrections to an earlier position. The construction, which in the early stages was loose, becomes increasingly compact and closed. Those views on the outside (typified in fig. 9.2 by 35) which are not interlocked with accepted conceptions perish in oblivion.

The same dynamics which Külling describes are presented with reference to a quite different realm of scientific inquiry by W. J. Ouweneel in his book *The Fall of the Christian West*, which I quote at some length:

> In 1830 the English geologist Charles Lyell published the first of his three books on geology, which still form the foundation of the discipline. Lyell basically excluded from his deliberations the possibility of such catastrophes [reported in the Bible as the Flood (Gen 6–8), which imply the supernatural involvement of God and which were unacceptable to the burgeoning scientism of the time. He] . . . attempted to explain the rise of the different geological strata through processes which are still observable today. . . .
>
> Now it is a historical fact of considerable importance that these new insights were not essentially grounded in new scientific discoveries. These would come later, for when one is unconditionally bent on finding something, then something often crops up which appears to be the thing being looked for. . . .
>
> The impetus for development of the evolutionary conception of geology was, then, philosophical deliberations. That is highly significant. The point of departure of this new outlook was not changes in the facts but rather changes in the presuppositions with which the facts were regarded.
>
> It was just the same with Charles Darwin, who as a young man read Lyell's books and found an indirect answer for a question which had exercised him greatly. For he refused to accept the assumption that all living things had come from God's creative act; yet he could also not conceive of an alternative possibility. Now he became familiar with Lyell's ideas. In them he found the notion that our world must be very old, for the gradual formation of the geological strata would obviously have required a great deal of time.
>
> And it was precisely such long spans of time which Darwin would later require for his view of the origin of species. For the random development of life forms necessitated billions of years; otherwise Darwin's idea would have been absurd from the start.
>
> These notions exerted mutual influence on each other. Later Darwin published his theory of evolution—likewise not essen-

tially on the basis of new scientific discoveries, but rather based on philosophical considerations. . . .[14]

He was looking for another solution to the problem of "the origin of life," for he did not *want* to believe any more in creation. He had a long period of doubting his faith between the ages of twenty-two and twenty-nine, and during this time he read an essay by the English clergyman Thomas Robert Malthus on overpopulation.

Malthus taught that wars, famines, and epidemics were necessary, for that was the only way for overpopulation to be dealt with. There is, said Malthus, a struggle for existence, the survival of the strongest or the fittest. . . .

"And then it suddenly dawned on me," reported Darwin later. All at once he realized what the correct solution to his problem was. The next twenty years, until 1859, he spent gathering arguments for his new theory.

Do you see how Darwin's view originated? Actually, it originated in the same manner that science in general operates. Science begins not so much with making observations and then constructing a theory. Rather, it begins with a conception, with an idea.

Darwin's idea came from Malthus, and Darwin needed twenty years to gather arguments, as well as to push aside arguments not in line with his theory, until he finally published his views.

Perhaps he would have spent twenty more years on the same project, had Alfred Wallace not developed the same idea, which caused Darwin to publish his *On the Origin of the Species* in order to get his views out first.

Perhaps you have the erroneous notion that scientists are entirely rational persons who function totally objectively, who gather and organize facts in an unbiased fashion. Well, Darwin is not the only one who operated as he did: all scientists employ these methods.[15]

No less questionable than the process of initiating so-called "scientific knowledge" is the form and manner in which such knowledge customarily extends its influence. An eminently credible witness to this fact is the Nobel prize winner in physics, Max Planck: "A new scientific truth does not usually become dominant by convincing its opponents, who declare that they

---

14. W. J. Ouweneel, *Der Untergang des christlichen Abendlandes* (2d ed., Heykoop, The Netherlands, 1978), 25–27.

15. Ibid., 28–30.

are now correctly informed. Rather, the opponents gradually die off, and the coming generation is familiarized from the start with the truth."[16]

What Planck describes is based in two phenomena: academic "schools" composed of mentors with their adherents, and group dynamics. Without consideration of these two factors, any number of historical developments, such as the course of the Arian controversy in the fourth century, or the triumphant advance of Bultmann's theology in the twentieth, defy adequate explanation.[17]

In summary we may now state that every new round in the game of science begins with an intuition instead of observation and the results of investigation as one might expect. Only afterwards are observations made which appear to confirm the overall outline. Interpersonal relationships—academic "schools," relations between colleagues, and group dynamics—then lead the new idea toward dominance. After this, there is a process of partial acceptance and denial, of correction, confirmation, and supplementation. The result is stabilization of an edifice constructed entirely with hypotheses. The principle of stabilizing through corrugation, which the packing industry employs to good effect, is at work here.[18]

At the end of the process there is a conception. It ingeniously summarizes a number of such new ideas and confers on them the appearance of cogency. The conception is based not so much on the force of argument as on how well it lends itself to a creative synthetic whole. The conception is applauded. From then on new ideas bind to the structure, and everything moving outside of this conception appears to be obsolete or eccentric.

The game continues with new ideas which presuppose the conception. Thus arises the whole network of accepted premises of a scientific discipline. If some of those presuppositions which

16. Cited in W. Gitt, *"Das Fundament"*, in *Wissen und Leben* Vol. 7 (Neuhausen-Stuttgart, 1985), 48.

17. It would probably be profitable to investigate how it happened that in the 1960s, most of the West German university teaching positions in New Testament were occupied by students and friends of Rudolf Bultmann.

18. [Linnemann uses the image of packing cardboard which is crimped or crinkled in order to give it far more strength than a flat piece of the same material would ever have alone. The "corrugating" of a new idea by the process she describes has a comparable effect: the idea, which by itself at first would have been torn to pieces, eventually gains great strength.]

supported the new ideas and arguments supporting it fail, then the stability of the conception remains unaffected. The presuppositions merely recede to the background of consciousness; they are still preserved—one might say hermetically sealed.

Since every conception is a presupposition for new ideas—and the new ideas lead in turn to new conceptions—it is not possible to make fundamental adjustments by giving proof that a presupposition is invalid. Even critical analysis of such ideas simply becomes a component in the process of stabilization: The idea comes under pressure from arguments, and the counterarguments, whether advanced by the mastermind of the idea or by some other advocate, have a stabilizing effect.

Every rational argument can be refuted by a counterargument, assuming there is enough time to think it over. This is the way our (fallen) intellect functions when it is not grounded in the truth of the Word of God. Even when one succeeds in furnishing proof, based on undeniably solid new information and results, one is rarely in a position to hinder the influence of established conceptions in the area of so-called science. This can be demonstrated in the natural sciences in connection with the myth of evolution. This myth still constitutes, at least in the area of the natural sciences, the framework of thought. Yet the evolutionary starting point has meanwhile been called into question in whole areas of research. The evolutionary hypothesis, by science's own admission, has been shown to be untenable at the level of the preliminary hypotheses which support it, which in turn discredits the overarching hypothesis itself. If science were what it pretends to be—objective, neutral, obligated only to the truth, impartial—the logical consequences would have been drawn long ago.

Science and Research in Evangelical Theology

An understanding of how presuppositions and conceptions actually function in science is necessary to answer the question which this chapter poses: Are science and research in evangelical theology essential or impossible?

Placed in the framework of a theological discipline, an evangelical scholar can either fill a gap or occupy a fringe position. In filling a gap he contributes to the stabilization of the system and is therefore fully accepted. In the fringe position he will either fall into the oblivion reserved for those who do not support the system, or he must protect his work by interlocking it with adjoining conceptions, recasting his original starting point. Some examples will illustrate this:

> Adolf Schlatter filled a gap in New Testament studies as a knowledgeable rabbinic scholar. He was therefore basically accepted. But what he had to say in terms of spiritual insight, for example in his commentaries on the entire New Testament,[19] was not taken seriously, being disregarded as "unscientific."

> J. T. Beck remained an outsider from the critical point of view, and his work was not carried forth. Similarly, K. Bornhäuser's contribution was undeservingly pushed to the side.

> Martin Kähler, on the other hand, knew how to get along within the prevailing structures. But the price he paid for this was too high. He ceased to be loyal to the Scriptures. His book *The So-Called Historical [historische] Jesus and the Historical [geschichtliche], Biblical Christ* clearly operated within the limits of pure reason (Kant) and respected Lessing's "ugly ditch" between necessary truths of reason and contingent facts of history. The book could therefore continue to exercise influence—and prepared the way for Bultmann's program of demythologization.

The evangelical dedicated to scientific work is pulled in a number of directions. First, the scholar must legitimate work by connecting it to the complex of traditions which make up the discipline in which he works. He can expect recognition only to the extent that this connection is satisfactorily achieved. Even if concerned to maintain a distance from prevailing views, he can manage this with respect to no more than one of the prevailing conceptions through the presentation of a new outline with a restricted scope. Other conceptions must remain. Then the researcher must wait to see whether this outline stabilizes itself in the course of science's progress, or whether it is disqualified because it is judged eccentric from the standpoint of the prevailing conception. To the extent that the outline is positively

---

19. Adolf Schlatter, *Erläuterungen zum Neuen Testament.*

received it will likely be made to conform to prevailing conceptions in the process of "stabilization through corrugation" referred to above.

Second, this person stands under the compulsion which understands science as a continually ascending march of progress. While this idea of progress has today generally faded into the background as a major feature in the modern worldview, it still reigns in scientific research with nearly unchecked force as an inherent obligation to show that progress is being made. Anyone who says "Yes" to science by conducting research can hardly escape the endless spiral of progress for progress' sake. The compulsion to show that progress is being made, however, and loyalty to what the Bible says are not compatible. Progress for the sake of progress will inevitably result in the desecration of God's Word.

Third, the researcher is pressured to make a name and thereby to seek honor.

Fourth, to claim that work is scientific, is to become subject to the criteria of assessment of historical-critical theology. What is "scientific" is decided, rightly or wrongly, by what has established itself in the general consciousness as science.

In scientific debate during the 1960s the question was raised whether theology could be called a science, since it is, after all, not presuppositionless. The question was answered by pointing out that theology makes use of the methods of historical and literary science and therefore must be recognized as a science just as they.

If evangelical theology makes the claim to be science, then it must ask itself if it wishes to use these methods to deal with God's Word. If it does so in an unrestricted fashion, then it has ceased to be evangelical. If it makes only restricted use of the methods, then it must reckon with being recognized as scientific to only a limited extent. It is not we evangelicals, but rather historical-critical theologians, who determine what is scientific.

Any evangelical who claims to be scientific hands himself over to the criteria of selection of historical-critical theology and must put up with being stigmatized as underqualified. For the concept of theological science is currently defined by historical-critical theology. To want to be "scientific" as a theologian inevitably means to know and accept one's place within the complex of traditions of a theological discipline.

Evangelicals and the Universities

Based on these observations, it seems obvious that it would be better to leave the theology faculties of the universities, in which historical-critical theology has become an institution, just as Abraham left the pagan environment of Ur in Chaldea because of God's call. We do not know, admittedly, the land we are going out to enter, but Abraham did not know, either, when he set out in obedience to God.

"Leaving" does not only mean to seek employment outside the theology faculties of state universities. In this respect most evangelicals do not face a decision, for they are not wanted in nor hired for university positions in the first place. "Leaving" means giving up the claim of being scientific, as well.

Claiming to be scientific means to regard the principles of science as foundational alongside God's Word. But these principles—seen in the light of God's Word—turn out to be inimical to God when used in this way. The claim to be scientific is a violation of the first commandment and results in the situation against which our fathers took a courageous stand with the first thesis of the Barmen Declaration.[20]

But giving up the claim to be scientific does not mean giving up competent intellectual work in theology. I believe that there can and should be scholarship on which God smiles and which God's people find helpful. Such scholarship is not some free-wheeling indulgence of intellectual curiosity which pries into everything that can be investigated. It takes its bearings, rather, from that which needs to be taught. It does not see itself as a means for selfish self-realization but rather as a ministry. Such scholarship is not caught in the pressure to which scientific work must submit:

First, such scholarship is not compelled to connect organically

---

20. [The Barmen Declaration was a statement issued in May 1934 by German church leaders. It renounced Christian complicity in and collaboration with the Third Reich. The "first thesis" cited by Linnemann includes these words: "Jesus Christ, as he is testified to us in the Holy Scripture, is the one Word of God, whom we are to hear, whom we are to trust and obey in life and in death. We repudiate the false teaching that the church can and must recognize yet other happenings and powers, images and truths as divine revelation alongside this one Word of God, as a source of her preaching." ET, John H. Leith, Creeds of the Church, (3d ed., Atlanta: John Knox, 1982), 520.]

with the complex of traditions in a discipline. It is necessary only to maintain the closest possible connection to God's Word.

Second, such scholarship is not determined by the obligation to show that scientific progress is being made. It is determined rather by the willingness to be like a "teacher of the law who has been instructed about the kingdom of heaven" and who "like the owner of a house . . . brings out of his storehouse new treasures as well as old" (Matt. 13:52).

Third, such scholarship is not under the compulsion to make a name for itself. Its passion is rather the willingness humbly to serve the body of Christ, using the gifts of God wherever God should see fit.

Fourth, along with the necessary agreement with God's Word, there is the criterion of judgment consisting solely in the quality of brotherly service in its function for the body of Christ. This service should contribute to, among other things, teaching, correction, edification, passing on beneficial information, and defending our most holy faith.

10

The Word of God

God's Word Is Inspired

Holy Scripture testifies explicitly to its origin in God in two passages. The first is 2 Timothy 3:16–17: "All Scripture is God-breathed and is useful for teaching, rebuking, correcting and training in righteousness, so that the man of God may be thoroughly equipped for every good work." The second testimony is 2 Peter 1:19–21: "And we have the word of the prophets made more certain, and you will do well to pay attention to it, as to a light shining in a dark place, until the day dawns and the morning star rises in your hearts. Above all, you must understand that no prophecy of Scripture came about by the prophet's own interpretation. For prophecy never had its origin in the will of man, but men spoke from God as they were carried along by the Holy Spirit."

These two testimonies do not assert merely "that God's Spirit, God's wisdom, has gone into these writings."[1] They can also not be restricted to mean only that the writers of Scripture experienced Romans 8:14[2] and that accordingly God's Spirit stood by and helped with the composition of the New Testament documents in the same way that he is with all believers in all of life.[3] The Greek Word *theopneustos* used in 2 Timothy 3:16 does not

---

1. Joachim Cochlovius, "*Leben aus dem Wort. Wege zu einem geistlichen Schriftverständnis,*" in J. Cochlovius and P. Zimmerling, eds., *Arbeitsbuch Hermeneutik* (Krelingen, 1983), 403–430 (here 411f.). I should point out that I am opposing only certain aspects of the position stated in this essay and by no means the entire essay. Still less am I directing criticism at the author himself.

2. ["... because those who are led by the Spirit of God are sons of God."]

3. Cochlovius, "*Leben aus dem Wort,*" 411.

mean "breathing God's spirit"[4] but rather "breathed into by God." There is a vast difference. What the verse states is that God is the originator of the Scriptures.

The biblical writers did not become "error-free and infallible persons,"[5] not even "during the period of the composition of their writings,"[6] but rather they *"spoke from God* as they were carried along by the Holy Spirit."

God's Word itself clearly declares God's Holy Spirit to be the originator of the Scriptures. The inspiration of Scripture is asserted by Scripture itself. The doctrine of inspiration is therefore no "unnecessary protective wall around the Bible,"[7] but rather the normative summary statement of what God's Word says about itself. This is not derived "from Rom. 8:14 and related passages"[8] but rather primarily from 2 Timothy 3:16–17 and 2 Peter 1:19–21. There "a special leading of the Spirit for the purpose of writing the Biblical books"[9] is explicitly claimed to have been at work. One stands in contradiction to the Holy Scripture, therefore, if one declares this claim to be "unnecessary and dubious from a Biblical and theological point of view."[10]

Verbal and Personal Inspiration

In testifying to its inspired status, Holy Scripture extends this status simultaneously to both the words (verbal inspiration) and the authors (personal inspiration). The evidence for *verbal inspiration* is 2 Timothy 3:16–17. This passage speaks of the *result* of inspiration: "All Scripture is God-breathed and is useful for teaching, rebuking, correcting and training in righteousness." Nothing is excluded; there is not one word in all of Scripture to which inspiration does not apply.

The evidence for *personal inspiration* is found in 2 Peter 1:19–21. This passage has in view the *manner* of inspiration, "men spoke from God as they were carried along by the Holy Spirit." Inspiration occurred as they were directed by the Holy Spirit from within, not according to mechanical dictation.

4. Ibid.
5. Ibid., 412.
6. Ibid.
7. Ibid.
8. Ibid.
9. Ibid.
10. Ibid.

Verbal inspiration is, therefore, not an idea that sprang up in the sixteenth century. It is attested by the Holy Scriptures and for that reason advocated by the church fathers. Verbal inspiration and personal inspiration are not competing doctrinal theories between which we must choose; they are, rather, two aspects of the same fact which God's Word conveys to us.

One needs to distinguish verbal inspiration from the verbal dictation theory that did arise in the sixteenth century. This was an unsuccessful human attempt to explain the doctrine of verbal inspiration. The correct doctrine of personal inspiration stands in conflict with the mechanical dictation theory but not with verbal inspiration. When a conception of personal inspiration conflicts with verbal inspiration, the doctrine of inspiration has been misunderstood and is out of line with Scripture.

Denials of Inspiration

Loyalty to God's Word also rules out the contention that Scripture "is not identical with God's word, for God's word is eternal, while Scripture is temporal."[11] By means of inspiration God has taken the Word spoken and written by men out of temporality.

In addition to the two chief witnesses (2 Tim. 3:16–17 and 2 Pet. 1:19–21), we find on almost every page of the Bible the assertion that it is God's Word, or Holy Scripture. When we do not extend our faith to what the Bible says about itself, we are not only contradicting God's Word; we are also declaring God himself, the originator of Scripture, to be a liar. We also stand in opposition to the one who is himself the Word (John 1:1–14) and who is called "Faithful and True" (Rev. 19:11). He is "the way and the truth and the life" (John 14:6). He is accordingly also the standard for what truth is: "Everyone on the side of truth listens to me" (John 18:37).

Should I be a professor, a pastor, or a high church official and not place my faith in God? Can I serve him when I do not believe what he says? That would be to treat him like a father whom I remind at every turn: "You're old; I've lost my respect for you; I am not bound by what you say." God is our Creator, and we live because of that grace in which he gave Jesus for us. Anyone who supposes that he can take such disrespectful liber-

11. Ibid.

ties with God's Word should heed the warning: "Do not be deceived: God cannot be mocked" (Gal. 6:7).

Perhaps there are readers whose eyes have now been opened. You did not realize what you were doing; you were just handling God's Word as you had been taught. This is a great day for you! You can turn aside from your perverse ways. God is merciful and gracious. He waits with open arms for everyone who will turn to him. He forgives readily for Jesus' sake.

Historical-critical theology says, "We cannot regard the Bible as Holy Scripture. Rather, at best we can only regard it as a book which claims to be Holy Scripture. There are other books which make the same claim, among them the Koran and the Vedas. Let us, then, disregard this claim and approach the Bible like any other book."

It is true that other books make such claims. Does this compel us to see the Bible as one scripture among many? Shall we compare it with the Veda or the Koran in order to determine whether the Bible is perhaps here and there just a bit superior? That is what historical-critical theology does. This is, however, a perverse procedure. In the same way that the "gods" of all the nations are not gods at all (1 Chron. 16:26; Ps. 96:5 and 97:7 and Jer. 2:11, 5:7), the sacred scriptures of other religions which claim to be revelatory are not Scripture at all. I know that our urbane upbringing which prizes tolerance above all else rebels against such a position. We respect, love, and value highly those around us, and what they regard as holy we wish to honor, too. But I stand by my statement, for it is true. If, according to God's Word, the gods of the nations are not gods at all, then the conclusion is inescapable that their sacred scriptures, which make revelatory claims, are not Scripture. For they do not reveal the one true God, who is not only the Creator of heaven and earth but also the Father of our Lord Jesus Christ, who moreover, together with the Son and the Holy Spirit, comprises the one triune God. Other scriptures cannot point the way to salvation.

When we permit ourselves to be pulled down to the level that we compare all the "Holy Scriptures" with each other so that we can perhaps grant that the Bible has a relative preeminence, then we are guilty of worshiping false gods. Let us learn from God's Word how mighty our God is and how contemptible and foolish this sort of false worship.

Isaiah 40:12–17 gives us an informative portrait of our God:

> Who has measured the waters in the hollow of his hand, or
> with the breadth of his hand marked off the heavens? Who has
> held the dust of the earth in a basket, or weighed the mountains
> on the scales and the hills in a balance? Who has understood the
> mind of the LORD, or instructed him as his counselor? Whom did
> the LORD consult to enlighten him, and who taught him the right
> way? Who was it that taught him knowledge or showed him the
> path of understanding? Surely the nations are like a drop in a
> bucket; they are regarded as dust on the scales; he weighs the
> islands as though they were fine dust. Lebanon is not sufficient
> for altar fires, nor its animals enough for burnt offerings. Before
> him all the nations are as nothing; they are regarded by him as
> worthless and less than nothing.

The same passage places the foolishness of worshiping false
gods before our eyes. In the context "gods" are being worshiped
which man himself has made: "To whom, then, will you compare God? What image will you compare him to? As for an idol,
a craftsman casts it, and a goldsmith overlays it with gold and
fashions silver chains for it. A man too poor to present such an
offering selects wood that will not rot. He looks for a skilled
craftsman to set up an idol that will not topple" (Isa. 40:18–20).

How can anyone compare the living God with the sorry imitations of men? He is not only the Creator; he is also the Lord
our God, the Almighty, who reigns. He sustains the entire cos-
mos at every moment and guides all that takes place in it:

> Do you not know? Have you not heard? Has it not been told
> you from the beginning? Have you not understood since the
> earth was founded? He sits enthroned above the circle of the
> earth, and its people are like grasshoppers. He stretches out the
> heavens like a canopy, and spreads them out like a tent to live in.
> He brings princes to naught and reduces the rulers of this world
> to nothing. No sooner are they planted, no sooner are they sown,
> no sooner do they take root in the ground, than he blows on
> them and they wither, and a whirlwind sweeps them away like
> chaff. "To whom will you compare me? Or who is my equal?"
> says the Holy One. Lift your eyes and look to the heavens: Who
> created all these? He who brings out the starry host one by one,
> and calls them each by name. Because of his great power and
> mighty strength, not one of them is missing. [Isa. 40:21–26]

Moreover, it is only our God who guides the course of the
future, and it is accordingly only he who is in a position to pro-

claim that which lies in the future. In this respect, as well, the gods of the nations turn out to be no gods at all: "'Present your case,' says the LORD. 'Set forth your arguments,' says Jacob's King. 'Bring in your idols to tell us what is going to happen. Tell us what the former things were, so that we may consider them and know their final outcome. Or declare to us the things to come, tell us what the future holds, so we may know that you are gods. Do something, whether good or bad, so that we will be dismayed and filled with fear. But you are less than nothing and your works are utterly worthless; he who chooses you is detestable'" (Isa. 41:21–24).

Whoever holds the Word of God—the Word of the Creator of heaven and earth, the Lord, our God, the Almighty, who reigns, the Father of our Lord Jesus Christ—whoever holds God's Word as basically comparable to the "sacred scriptures" of other religions is guilty of the worship of false gods. He pulls God down to the level of the false gods.

We see, then, that comparing God's Word to other "scriptures" using this sort of comparative approach—which is fundamental to historical-critical theology—amounts to an abominable worship of false gods. Such a comparison tolerates other gods in addition to God and confers on them the same honor.

Freedom from Error

As the inspired Word of God, holy Scripture is free from error, not only in the area of faith and life but also in all other areas. At a point where some problem arises God's Word is valid and not our presumed insight.

God himself states: "I am watching to see that my Word is fulfilled" (Jer. 1:12). Would he not also have watched over his Word as it was written down and the various writings collected? God's Word also states: "The king's heart is in the hand of the LORD; he directs it like a watercourse wherever he pleases" (Prov. 21:1). Would he not have protected the hearts of those he inspired from inserting error or misstatement into Holy Scripture as a result of limited human knowledge and insight? Who dares to impute powerlessness or neglect to God in this matter?

In 2 Timothy 3:16–17 it is asserted clearly that Holy Scripture contains nothing erroneous or false. Otherwise it could hardly be said that *"all Scripture* is God-breathed and is useful for teaching, rebuking, correcting and training in righteousness." Error and falsehood could not serve such a purpose. How can we dare to allege that there are errors in God's Word in some area of natural science, or history, or some other discipline—we, whose scientific findings of yesterday and the day before are already outdated today? Woe to us if we possess such audacity! Should we not be thoroughly ashamed to say, "Here is an error in God's Word"? How do we intend to endure the flaming eyes of Jesus one day when our learned books which propagate such things are consumed like chaff? Let us turn back from such a disastrous course and take refuge in our Savior Jesus Christ!

God's Word saw through contemporary theology long ago. Isaiah 32:5 alludes to a situation in which the common person (literally "the fool," which refers not to someone who lacks intelligence but rather to someone who rejects God's authority) is called noble and the worst of scoundrels and deceivers is highly respected. Are we ourselves not godless fools when we handle God's Word as if there were no God? Yet that is exactly what historical-critical theology does! Are we not malicious deceivers when we falsify God's Word by our approach to Scripture so that the congregation no longer receives it as flawless and pure? Those theologians, however, who fraudulently alter the Word of God, so that church members get stones instead of bread and poison instead of water, are today hailed as noble; they are regarded as honorable scientists; they find recognition in the church and in the world. They are accorded high status. They receive titles. They become doctors and professors and are often even named as bishops.

But God's Word says of such individuals, "For the fool speaks folly, his mind is busy with evil. He practices ungodliness and spreads error concerning the LORD; the hungry he leaves empty and from the thirsty he withholds water. The scoundrel's methods are wicked, he makes up evil schemes to destroy the poor with lies, even when the plea of the needy is just" (Isa. 32:6–7).

The present situation offers an exact analogy: God's Word, adulterated by historical criticism, leaves the souls of the hungry empty. The drink of life-giving water, of the living Word of God, is withheld from the thirsty. When a meek person who has been humbly instructed by God's Word sets forth what he has every right to, he is utterly opposed—in the name of science. As far as credentials go he is a pauper: He has not completed formal study, possesses no title, and can produce no proof of passing examinations before a human authority.

But things do not have to remain this way, for our Savior Jesus has appeared: "See, a king will reign in righteousness and rulers will rule with justice. Each man will be like a shelter from the wind and a refuge from the storm, like streams of water in the desert and the shadow of a great rock in a thirsty land. Then the eyes of those who see will no longer be closed, and the ears of those who hear will listen. The mind of the rash will know and understand, and the stammering tongue will be fluent and clear. No longer will the fool be called noble nor the scoundrel be highly respected" (Isa. 32:1–5).

Let us, by God's grace, acquire knowledge and become truly noble persons who make noble plans and stand by noble deeds (Isa. 32:8). Then the souls of the hungry will not remain empty. Water will not be withheld from the thirsty. The meek will no longer be destroyed by lies.

God's Word Is Homogeneous

The Word of God is homogenous and unified; it is entirely and totally God's Word. To classify its various parts according to our own evaluation system is insolence. It is, nevertheless, standard procedure in historical-critical theology to accord different levels of validity to different portions of God's Word. A few portions of Holy Scripture are made into a yardstick to assess and devalue the rest. In this way one searches for a "canon within the canon" and uses the critical method referred to as *Sachkritik*.

We will cite two examples of this: In the first, the so-called *realized eschatology* in John's Gospel is played off against the *futuristic eschatology* in the three other Gospels, the so-called synoptics. But in order to do this one has to account for the presence of statements in John's gospel which do not fit in with the alleged realized eschatology. This requires a hypothetical "ecclesiastical redactor" who is supposed to have inserted verses that conflict with John's own outlook.

In the second example, the christological statements in Romans are played off against the so-called *cosmic christology* of Ephesians and Colossians. This allows Ephesians and Colossians to be set aside as non-Pauline and therefore inferior since Paul's own writings rank higher than what is *deuteropauline*.

When the enemy cannot divert us totally from the Word, he attempts to trick us using the presumptuousness of our own evaluation. He succeeded in this even with Martin Luther, who devalued James by calling it "an epistle of straw" and has been made the star witness for historical-critical theology. Let us be alert, for our "enemy the devil prowls around like a roaring lion looking for someone to devour" (1 Peter 5:8).

Whoever uses *Sachkritik* to select from God's Word what he regards as normative is like the person who builds an idol. He creates for himself that which he worships. What foolishness—a mere human, who requires meat and drink for subsistence, undertakes to create a god. He creates this god in his own image, reflecting human limitations, using, of course, the raw material of the God who made heaven and earth and even the person as well. The same material needed for the satisfaction of bodily needs is used to create a god to worship:

> All who make idols are nothing, and the things they treasure are worthless. Those who would speak up for them are blind; they are ignorant, to their own shame. Who shapes a god and casts an idol, which can profit him nothing? He and his kind will be put to shame; craftsmen are nothing but men. Let them all come together and take their stand; they will be brought down to terror and infamy.
>
> The blacksmith takes a tool and works with it in the coals; he shapes an idol with hammers, he forges it with the might of his arm. He gets hungry and loses his strength; he drinks no water and grows faint. The carpenter measures with a line and makes an outline with a marker; he roughs it out with chisels and marks it with compasses. He shapes it in the form of man, of man in all his glory, that it may dwell in a shrine. He cut down cedars, or perhaps took a cypress or oak. He let it grow among the trees of the forest, or planted a pine, and the rain made it grow. It is man's fuel for burning; some of it he takes and warms himself, he kindles a fire and bakes bread. But he also fashions a god and worships it; he makes an idol and bows down to it. Half of the wood he burns in the fire; over it he prepares his meal, he roasts his meat and eats his fill. He also warms himself and says, "Ah! I am warm; I see the fire." From the rest he makes a god, his idol; he bows down to it and worships. He prays to it and says, "Save me; you are my god" [Isa. 44:9–17].

Am I not just an idolater if I form my God from earth or stone or wood? Am I not also an idolater if I use God's Word like a vein of ore, or a stone quarry, or a stand of timber to cut down? When I take from God's Word what seems good to me and depend on my human reason to assemble a god in the image of my own limited insight, is this not idolatry?

The same understanding with which a person chooses a car to buy, finances a house, decides whether to install gas or electric heat, and earns his living must suffice to create a god. But God says, "I am the LORD; that is my name! I will not give my glory to another or my praise to idols" (Isa. 42:8). Or again: "But those who trust in idols, who say to images, 'You are our gods,' will be turned back in utter shame" (Isa. 42:17). Is it likely that one can depend on such a homemade god when divine deliverance is really needed? Certainly not! May anyone who handles God's Word in this fashion ponder whether he is really trusting God, or whether he is not rather seeking security in the things of this world.

May it shock and frighten us that such idolatry is so widespread today among God's people. Let us heed God's lament: "'But my people have exchanged their Glory for worthless idols. Be appalled at this, O heavens, and shudder with great horror,' declares the LORD. 'My people have committed two sins: They have forsaken me, the spring of living water, and have dug their own cisterns, broken cisterns that cannot hold water'" (Jer. 2:11–13).

Let us reverse course if we are headed in the wrong direction. Let us ask God to show us our error. It is often through very small beginnings that we get off track. The error can at first be minor indeed, but it gradually comes to light that we have struck out in the wrong direction—here a couple of statements crossed out in God's Word, there a shrug of the shoulders, now a reservation, the acceptance of a few critical thoughts which suggest themselves as answers to problems which we have or we have been talked into having. Suddenly the Bible is for us no longer entirely the sacred Word of the living God.

Let us go to the cross if we have erred. Our Lord Jesus shed his blood for this sin, too.

God's inspired Word, which has many human authors but ultimately only one divine originator, exhibits a wonderful unity. As soon as I accept by faith the self-testimony of the Word of God regarding the inspiration of Scripture, I begin to realize this wondrous unity. How glorious is the framework of promises relating to our Lord and Savior Jesus Christ and the fulfillment of those promises. How precious is the agreement between Ezekiel 16 and Luke 15, between John 10:1–18 and Ezekiel 34:11–16. How wonderful is all that is brought together in Revelation, much of it already foretold in advance by the Old Testament prophets. A veil obscures the vision of some to all this, so that they cannot see it (see 2 Cor 3:14–15), but the Holy Spirit opens up God's Word to him who is no longer disobedient to it.

The person who does not wish to see God's Word as a unity having one originator, in which each part complements the other, but rather views it as an anthology of disparate writers whose profiles one must toil to work out—that person cannot apprehend the unity of God's Word. He attempts to pit the New Testament against the Old Testament, Paul against James, Genesis 1 against Genesis 2, 1 Corinthians 15 against John 5. He alleges that Genesis 2 has a different concept of God than 1 Kings 18 and that the God of which Jesus spoke was not the same as the God of the Old Testament.

As already stated, the reason for such erroneous judgments is that one starts out with a conceptualization of God which, as a product of the human imagination, is too small to contain the entire fullness of the self-revelation of God in his Word. In addition, there is quite often a lack of thorough awareness of the entire Word of God due to the extreme specialization which is an established feature of theological and biblical criticism. For anyone who truly knows the Old Testament and does not just have some haphazard conception of it, it is quite impossible to pit it against the New Testament and vice versa.

God's Word Is Consistent

The Word of God is consistent in its message through the ages. One of the great lies of the enemy, one he uses to drive persons away from God's Word, is the doctrine that humanity is historically determined. It is claimed that human fate is wrapped up in whatever time period is at hand. Faith conceptions for one generation are quite different from those for the previous generations, since the external circumstances have altered and technological progress has occurred. In this view it matters little whether the progress is from crude knife to sickle for grain harvesting, or from mowing machine to combine. It is simply maintained that every generation must discover its own access to God, its own interpretation of Scripture, and its own doctrine of Christ. It is maintained that God's Word requires ongoing reinterpretation in the light of this state of affairs. What was once valid is regarded as obsolete, and this includes the Word of God. There used to be other means of production and other societal conditions; we can therefore not take God's Word literally as it stands before our eyes on the page. We can accept it, rather, only by an interpretive process which highlights that which (still) holds relevance for us.

God's Word, however, says the same thing to persons of the twentieth century as it did to those of the first. Man stands before God today in no other way than he did a couple of thousand years ago. The means of production of the technological age have not altered man's essential makeup. As it was in the days of Lot and Noah, so it is still today: people eat, they drink, they buy, they plant, they marry and are given in marriage (see Luke 17:27–30). It is said that one cannot expect the modern person to believe in resurrection from the dead and miracles, in angels and demons, for this is the age of technology, of radio and the refrigerator, of electric lights and autos. Yet precisely this same modern person now succumbs to superstitions the likes of which we have not seen in centuries. Many trust in amulets and horoscopes and seek direction from seers. Involvement with satanic cults is definitely on the rise.

God's Word knows man, yes, even contemporary man. And God has already prophesied in his Word the sense in which contemporary man differs from man of bygone eras:

> But mark this: There will be terrible times in the last days. People will be lovers of themselves, lovers of money, boastful, proud, abusive, disobedient to their parents, ungrateful, unholy, without love, unforgiving, slanderous, without self-control, brutal, not lovers of the good, treacherous, rash, conceited, lovers of pleasure rather than lovers of God—having a form of godliness but denying its power. Have nothing to do with them.
>
> They are the kind who worm their way into homes and gain control over weak-willed women, who are loaded down with sins and are swayed by all kinds of evil desires, always learning but never able to acknowledge the truth. Just as Jannes and Jambres opposed Moses, so also these men oppose the truth—men of depraved minds, who, as far as the faith is concerned, are rejected. [2 Tim. 3:1–8]

The thesis that God's Word is dependent on interpretation and that every generation needs its own interpretation stands in opposition to the truth. The necessity of interpreting God's Word is an artifice of historical-critical theology, which does not want to accept the Word as it stands and therefore must expend much effort. Since this theology also does not wish to view God's Word as a unity, it cannot make use of the principle that Scripture is its own interpreter. And since it does not regard the Holy Spirit as the originator of Scripture, it cannot experience him as interpreter. In addition, historical-critical theology is hindered by ignorance, since the theologian generally is only aware of those small parts of the Bible which he regularly studies in keeping with the widespread tendency to specialize. As a rule he knows numerous books that deal with his area of interest, but he does not know his Bible.

We do not wish to neglect to mention, however, that teachers who are true to the Bible, who instruct us in God's Word, are a gift of God's grace (Eph. 4:11). We do not want to scorn their service and the assistance which their books offer.

God's Word Was Revealed

God's Word is the product of progressive revelation. Abraham and Noah did not yet have the law, and our Lord Jesus said of the prophets and righteous persons of the Old Covenant: "For I tell you the truth, many prophets and righteous men longed to see what you see but did not see it, and to hear what you hear but did not hear it" (Matt. 13:17). "The law is only a shadow of the good things that are coming—not the realities themselves" (Heb. 10:1). Earthly and heavenly Jerusalem must be distinguished from each other (Gal. 4:25–27), and one must observe what is written for the descendents of Abraham according to the flesh, on the one hand, and what for the children of promise, on the other (Rom. 4:16, Gal. 4:28). God's Word must be handled accurately (2 Tim. 2:15). We must keep God's overarching redemptive scheme in view.

God's Word itself gives us instructions so that we can read it aright: "All Scripture is God-breathed and is useful for teaching, rebuking, correcting and training in righteousness . . ." (2 Tim. 3:16). It teaches us how we are to understand the accounts contained in the Old Testament:

For I do not want you to be ignorant of the fact, brothers, that our forefathers were all under the cloud and that they all passed through the sea. They were all baptized into Moses in the cloud and in the sea. They all ate the same spiritual food and drank the same spiritual drink; for they drank from the spiritual rock that accompanied them, and that rock was Christ. Nevertheless, God was not pleased with most of them; their bodies were scattered over the desert.

Now these things occurred as examples to keep us from setting our hearts on evil things as they did. Do not be idolaters, as some of them were; as it is written: "The people sat down to eat and drink and got up to indulge in pagan revelry." We should not commit sexual immorality, as some of them did—and in one day twenty-three thousand of them died. We should not test the Lord, as some of them did—and were killed by snakes. And do not grumble, as some of them did—and were killed by the destroying angel.

These things happened to them as examples and were written down as warnings for us, on whom the fulfillment of the ages has come. [1 Cor. 10:1–11]

We are also instructed to seek Christ in the Scriptures. "That rock was Christ," says 1 Corinthians 10:4. "You search the Scriptures because you think that in them you have eternal life; and it is these that bear witness of me" (John 5:39, NASB).

God's Word makes it plain enough what it is there for and how we may make proper use of it: "For everything that was written in the past was written to teach us, so that through endurance and the encouragement of the Scriptures we might have hope" (Rom. 15:4). If we follow these instructions we will handle God's Word aright and the diligent study of Scripture will be fruitful.

God's Word Is Sufficient

God's Word is enough; it is completely and entirely sufficient for every person, for every age, for every situation. "The streams of God are filled with water" (Ps. 65:9). We can never exhaust God's Word. Situations of which the writers of the Word of God could have known nothing were taken into consideration by God's Spirit. Things of which we still had no knowledge a few years back were already written down two or three thousand years ago. As was said in Daniel 12:8–9: "I heard, but I did not understand. So I asked, 'My lord, what will the outcome of all this be?' He replied, 'Go your way, Daniel, because the words are closed up and sealed until the time of the end.'"

The Word of God requires no supplementation, either through psychology or depth psychology or through modern educational theory. God's Word knows man better than either psychology or depth psychology is able to know him. Where the findings of these disciplines contain elements of truth, these were already accessible long ago in God's Word. For the most part, however, psychology and depth psychology possess an anti-Christian character and stand in opposition to God's Word.

In instances where someone has felt compelled to contradict God's Word due to having better insight and greater mercy—for example in the question of premarital intercourse, or of marriage and divorce—all that has ultimately resulted is untold misery. The same goes for modern educational theory. Many have supposed they could help children by turning away from the principles of child-rearing which God's Word teaches us. Meanwhile, the products of such education make it clear enough that God knows better what benefits society. God's Word says, for example: "Folly is bound up in the heart of a child, but the rod of discipline will drive it far from him" (Prov. 22:15). "Do not withhold discipline from a child; if you punish him with the rod, he will not die. Punish him with the rod, and save his soul from death" (Prov. 23:13–14). "He who spares the rod hates his son, but he who loves him is careful to discipline him" (Prov. 13:24).

Modern educational theory claims to know better than this. It says children must not undergo corporal punishment, certainly not with "the rod." Today some even go so far as to maintain that it is better not to discipline children at all, but rather to let them develop however they please. But look at what a generation of young fools we have already produced, young people who are incapable of assuming responsibility and leading a normal human life. They cannot resist giving in to whatever feeling of carnal pleasure, or displeasure, they experience. Many fall prey to drugs and alcohol, some even dying from overdose and others finally landing in asylums.

God's Word also does not need supplementation from sociology. God knows more about man and his various social relations than our rational deductions can fathom. Neither does God's

Word stand in need of correction from the natural sciences. It turns out that the views of natural science which formerly were used to discredit the Bible have now been proven invalid by more recent scientific developments.

Let us, like the young Daniel, dispense with the diet offered by the world as a side dish to God's Word. We will surely not be malnourished compared to those to eat from the king's diet of worldly wisdom (Dan. 1:10). We will rather be superior to the learned in matters of insight and wisdom (Dan. 1:20). "Every Word of God is flawless; he is a shield to those who take refuge in him. Do not add to his words, or he will rebuke you and prove you a liar" (Prov. 30:5).

God's Word also needs no augmenting from our experience. Experiences which have no precedent *in* the Word of God have no business trying to legitimate themselves *from* the Word of God. Even the exercise of the gifts of the Holy Spirit is to be rejected if it adds something to the Word of God by claiming to generate revelatory prophecies equal in authority to it.

God's Word Is Effective

"For he spoke, and it came to be; he commanded, and it stood firm" (Ps. 33:9). But this effectiveness manifests itself only where the Word as it stands is simply accepted in faith. That is why so many miracles happen in places where the age-old, cynical "Did God really say?" (Gen 3:1), generated today by theological, psychological, sociological, and historical-critical skepticism, has not yet penetrated. That is why persons who simply place faith in God's Word experience miracles even here in the West.

Two mistakes are to be avoided. Both are alluded to in James 4:2–3: "You do not have, because you do not ask God. When you ask, you do not receive, because you ask with wrong motives, that you may spend what you get on your pleasures."

The precondition for petition is being taught by and familiar with God's Word. I must know what God wishes to grant so that I can make request. Every impairment of God's Word through theological theories (for example, that God no longer wishes to work in certain ways today; that was only for the time of the apostles) or through critical assessment based on everyday experience has wide-ranging implications; "You do not have, because you do not ask God." Even giving room to doubt whether God wishes to grant something has fateful consequences. God's Word says: "But when he asks, he must believe and not doubt, because he who doubts is like a wave of the sea, blown and tossed by the wind. That man should not think he will receive anything from the Lord; he is a double-minded man, unstable in all he does" (James 1:6–8). By lack of expectancy we hinder God from giving us what he would like to bestow and what he has accordingly promised in his Word. We hinder his Word so that it does not have the effect God would wish.

The other mistake consists in asking "with wrong motives." This is when we make demands of God as if we could sue him in order to collect on the promises he has made. When we stand before God like defiant, ill-mannered children who demand that we get what we want, longing first of all for the fulfillment of self-serving wishes rather than for his kingdom, then we force God to deny us that which he has promised in his Word. Once again we hinder his Word so that it does not have the effect he would wish.

God's Word Mirrors God

In his Word we can recognize God's heart and the principles that guide his actions. Here are two examples of this:

We can recognize how great are God's mercy and his saving love by noting how he dealt with Ahab. It had been said of Ahab: "There was never a man like Ahab, who sold himself to do evil in the eyes of the LORD, urged on by Jezebel his wife" (1 Kings 21:25). When Ahab inspected the vineyard which he acquired by murdering Naboth, the prophet Elijah confronted him to pronounce God's judgment on him and his house:

> When Ahab heard these words, he tore his clothes, put on sackcloth and fasted. He lay in sackcloth and went around meekly.
> Then the word of the Lord came to Elijah the Tishbite: "Have you noticed how Ahab has humbled himself before me? Because he has humbled himself, I will not bring this disaster in his day, but I will bring it on his house in the days of his son." [1 Kings 21:27–29]

Truly, when God calls us to be "slow to anger" (James 1:19), he is first that way himself.

The most overwhelming picture of God's character is seen in the mirror of 1 Corinthians 13:4–7: "Love is patient, love is kind. It does not envy, it does not boast, it is not proud. It is not rude, it is not self-seeking, it is not easily angered, it keeps no record of wrongs. Love does not delight in evil but rejoices with the truth. It always protects, always trusts, always hopes, always perseveres."

Let us search the Scriptures, and let us respond in such a way that we find in them the way to God's heart. True knowledge of Scripture leads to worship in spirit and truth.

Subject Index

161

Scripture Index